PRAISE

The *Stepmom's Guide* to

"This wonderful book is a balm to any stepmom who feels even the tiniest bit overwhelmed. And who among us doesn't?! With honesty, humor, and valuable exercises, Karon encourages us to make life-enhancing choices that can help keep the spark in our marriages and guide us toward fulfilling friendships with inherited children."

— Sue Patton Thoele, author, *The Courage to be a Stepmom: Finding Your Place Without Losing Yourself*

"Realistic, practical, and caring help for one of the most challenging tasks a woman can face. It's a 'must read' for any woman who is, or who is about to become, a stepmother."

— Robert H. Lauer, Ph.D., and Jeanette C. Lauer, Ph.D., co-authors, *Becoming Family: How to Build a Stepfamily that Really Works*

"This upbeat, no-nonsense guide looks at the difficult tasks involved in the making of a stepfamily and presents ways to handle them successfully. Karon's good advice will be welcomed not just by stepmoms but by *all* in the family."

— Claire Berman, former president, Stepfamily Association of America; author, *Making It as a Stepparent* and *What Am I Doing in a Stepfamily?*

"A dose of thoughtful, sensible, concrete reality—filled with practical, down-to-earth examples and suggestions—that can simplify unrealistic expectations and help blended families find more pleasure in everyday life."

— Alvin Rosenfeld, M.D., co-author, *The Over-Scheduled Child: Avoiding the Hyper-Parenting Trap*

"Strengthening our families is critical. Karon Phillips Goodman helps those of us with special challenges."

— Hadassah Lieberman, wife of U.S. Senator Joseph Lieberman and mother of four (birthed two, raised four)

"Simply put, this is one of the most useful books I have read about stepmothering. It will certainly become a 'must-have' on my list of recommended reading for stepmoms."

— Allison R. Rehor, founder, Mile-Hi Stepfamilies

"The reader feels as if she's sitting across the table sharing a chocolate dessert and some girl talk with the author. A realistic roadmap, with real-life strategies."

— Susie Michelle Cortright, founder & publisher, *Momscape.com*

"Karon Goodman takes complicated issues, gives choices, eliminates the impossible, and simply makes life easier. *Bride Again Magazine* recommends encore brides read this book before they say 'I do.'"

— Beth Reed Ramirez, publisher, *Bride Again*

"A mature, experienced, and straight-shooting reference. This book will empower and encourage all those involved in steplife."

— Christy Borgeld, founder, Stepfamily Day; board member, Stepfamily Association of America

"Save your sanity and keep your dignity intact with this common-sense approach to stepmothering! This book is a MUST HAVE! It touches so close to home, you'll feel it was written from your own personal experience."

— Christine D. Atwell, president, The Stepfamily Connection, Inc.

"A wonderfully supportive book for stepfamilies that blends excellent advice with heartfelt care and support."

— The Stepfamily Network

"Written with compassion, truth, humor, and love, it is a guide and workbook worthy of re-reading many times."

— BB Webb, stepparenting columnist, *The Barrow County (Ga.) News*

"A comforting companion; easy to read, funny, and wise."

— Judy Ford, L.C.S.W., family therapist; author, *Wonderful Ways to be a Stepparent* and *Wonderful Ways to Love a Child*

"An invaluable resource for all stepmothers, whether they are newlyweds or battle-weary veterans. I have just recently discovered the simplifying process Karon speaks of, but her book has made it so much easier!"

— Kim Peterson, founder, *FamilyFusion.com*

"Every stepmother's resource for saving sanity and spirit! Motivational, inspirational, and sensational!"

— Susan Wilkins-Hubley, founder, *www.secondwivesclub.com*

"The *Guide* comes not a moment too soon, as stepmoms everywhere sorely need a compassionate hand and heart to guide them. The 'Tales from the Blender' are both hilariously and heartwrenchingly familiar. What a great resource for the community of stepmoms out there."

—Astrid Scholz, Ph.D., president, StepTogether

"Karon offers sound, tangible solutions to everyday issues, with entertaining perspective and refreshing honesty. But don't expect a magic book of answers. The true beauty of this book is that it teaches you to find your own answers, which is infinitely more valuable!"

— Nicole L. Weyant, founder, *Step-Family-Matters.com*

"Stepparenting will always be challenging. Thank God there are resources like this book to offer a helping hand along the way."

— Azriela Jaffe, author, *Create Your Own Luck*, *mom of three, stepmom of two*

"What I liked most was how Karon related her personal experiences as a stepmom throughout the book. Karon's book is a must read for us all!"

— Mikki Forsyth, mom of three, stepmom of four

The
Stepmom's Guide to
Simplifying
Your Life

KARON PHILLIPS GOODMAN

Books that inform and inspire

© 2002 by Karon Phillips Goodman. All rights reserved. Except as permitted under the Copyright Act of 1976, no part of this book may be reproduced or transmitted in any form or by any means or stored in a data base or retrieval system, without written permission from the author.

Some of the names given in "Tales from the Blender" are pseudonyms.

Published by:
EquiLibrium Press, Inc.
10736 Jefferson Blvd. #680
Culver City, California 90230
USA
(310) 204-3290   fax (310) 204-3550
www.equipress.com

EquiLibrium Press logo and "Books that inform and inspire" are registered trademarks of EquiLibrium Press, Inc.

Cover and interior design: Mayapriya Long, www.bookwrights.com
Cover art: Corbis

Printed in the United States of America

Publisher's Cataloging-in-Publication
(Provided by Quality Books, Inc.)

Goodman, Karon Phillips.
    The stepmom's guide to simplifying your life / by Karon Phillips Goodman. — 1st ed.
        p. cm.
        Includes bibliographical references.
        LCCN 2001099476
        ISBN 0-9667393-7-X

    1. Stepmothers—Family relationships.
2. Stepfamilies. 3. Simplicity. 4. Conduct of Life.
I. Title.

HQ759.92.G66 2002   646.7'8
                                     QBI33-302

To my husband, Bill,
the reason I believe in the
power of things "meant to be."

Contents

While we may not be able to control all that happens to us, we can control what happens inside us.

— Benjamin Franklin

Introduction

Well, now you've really gone and done it. Just when you thought you had a clue about how to handle your life, you went and jumped in up to your neck.

You've married a man you love even more than long-lasting hair color. At the same time, you've become a parent to another woman's children, whether they welcome you or not. You now have more relatives than you know what to do with, and just getting through a weekend requires a Ph.D. in strategic planning.

Welcome to the world of the stepmother and second wife (and perhaps also mother and ex-wife). With all of these roles to fill, you've stopped trying to be Super Woman. You'll settle for being *Sane* Woman. Even that seems a lofty goal, considering the way you've complicated your life.

When you enter into a stepfamily, you become part of one of the most challenging kinds of family relationships. Your mind, your spirit, your patience, and your strength are tested time after time. As you overcome hurdles and sidestep hazards day in and day out, your life starts to feel like an endless obstacle course.

Believe me, I know. This book grows out of my experiences in a stepfamily that has seen both good days and bad, one that has survived the many traumas that come with the territory. I come to you humbled but enlightened, offering any help that I can give.

The words of wisdom that I wish to share weren't bequeathed from above as I sat meditating in the pristine quiet of early morning. No, I learned about stepfamily life the hard way. I come to you as a battered soldier, one who has earned her stripes, thank you very much. Sometimes I went into battle timidly—which was about as effective as waving a fly swatter at a grizzly bear. At other times I was merciless, as if pointing an assault rifle at a dandelion.

I struggled and cried and complained and contemplated felonies, until I came to the remarkable conclusion that I would be much happier—not to mention stay out of divorce court—if I somehow could *simplify* my life instead of *complicating* it more. I realized that the very quality of my life depended on finding a better way to meet its challenges, and I was determined to find a simpler path.

With that one decision, I regained all of the sanity and power I thought I had lost forever. I finally was able to focus on growth and possibilities, instead of loss and regret.

If you, too, have surveyed the colossal pile of challenges that awaits you each day and longed for a simpler life, please read on. If you have lost control of your life since you remarried, or if you fear that will happen, take heart. You, too, can overcome. You can discard the debris that lies knee-deep around you—the loss and the fear, the doubt and the pain. I know how overwhelming it can be, and I hope that you will find help, strength, and guidance here.

If you make the choice to simplify the parts of your life that you can control, and then manage them well, there not only is hope—there is a great probability that your stepfamily will succeed. If you are able to experience the rewards and blessings of stepmothering, this book will have served its purpose.

Before we get started, a few words of explanation:

A stepfamily is a group of unrelated people brought together by one very brave couple. Sometimes in this book, I refer to these unions as "blended families." Even though we know that perfect blending isn't possible in any stepfamily, I believe that your family can come together and share common goals and mutual respect. You can become more one family than two as each day passes. For that reason, I have chosen to alternate among the terms "family," "stepfamily," and "blended family."

Second, my focus is on the stepmom because she often is the spouse who is caught in the middle of nearly everything that happens in her family. She is hearth and home, yet she keeps time to another mom's schedule. She is nurse and nurturer, yet she is neither first nor favorite. However devoted she may be to her stepchildren, her embrace of them is interrupted by another mom's grasp. Although many dads in a stepfamily also are acutely aware of the difficulties, it is the stepmom who usually must deal with them so intimately, and for that reason, this book is addressed to her.

CHAPTER 1

Choose Simplicity

A stepfamily is a never-ending second chance. Make it count.

Before my son was born, I thought I was a busy person. Afterward, I wondered what I'd done with all the spare time I'd had before I was a mom. When I became a second wife and stepmom to two more sons one hot September afternoon, I again marveled at what used to be. How simple and uneventful my life must have been!

Compared to the tumultuous, pull-you-under-at-every-breath tidal wave that I was now living, my earlier life looked like a slow-motion seascape. Just by becoming a stepmom, my world, and my grasp on it, were turned upside down. Sometimes I felt as if I couldn't breathe, that there was no air around me.

I loved my husband more than anything, and our boys got along well. So I was stunned by how much my new marriage scared me. I felt fear and uncertainty at every turn. I was terrified of failing, but had no idea what to do to prevent it. When there was even the tiniest bump on the road I had mapped so carefully, I crumbled. Each imperfect moment became a reason to question myself. I often wondered what I had gotten myself into.

I now realize that many of our early problems were my fault, because I spent my time obsessing over the past, agonizing over the present, and desperately trying to control the future. I was never thankful for a small victory in the battle to become a "real" family—I wanted to win the war, immediately. When that didn't happen, I resolved to find a way to make it happen.

My insecurity was so tangible that at times it literally took my breath away. How would I ever make this work? What if I had been wrong? What if this marriage was the biggest mistake of my life?

I don't know if I believed that choosing a simpler life would save me, but I knew that I had to change. Either I had to find some peace in my life, or I would have to find a different life. My choices became very easy when I got to that point.

When I finally was able to step back, relax, and simplify my life, the same problems were still there. The kids still argued. My husband still failed to understand me now and then. My fears didn't disappear overnight. But at least I could breathe. Through the chaos, I could see promise and possibility.

My *life* hadn't changed; my *approach* to it had. Everything looked the same, but *I* was different. When I learned to appreciate more and control less, I was stronger. I now could truly believe that the health of my family didn't rest solely with me. When my approach changed, my life changed, too, for the better.

If you are a stepmom, you may know that frightening, suffocating feeling. The life you had before your marriage—the one you thought was so complex—must seem almost convent-like now. Any simplicity that you'd managed to incorporate into your life was obliterated when you arrived in a stepfamily. You said two tiny words and your life became about as simple as interplanetary travel. For better or worse, you will never be the same again.

The list of complications in a stepfamily is long and seems to gets longer all the time: stepsibling rivalry, finances that keep getting tighter, adjusting to the new people living in your home (whether full or part-time), worrying about your stepchildren's mom's impression of you and her influence on the kids, your parents' reactions to new grandkids, new in-laws, the relationship between your husband and your kids, the relationship between your husband and your ex-husband. . . . It just goes on and on, and that's on an easy day!

In a second (or subsequent) marriage, you'll work feverishly to turn all of these random-seeming elements into a family. It seems so implausible, but it's not impossible. By simplifying your choices, you can build a better, more satisfying life. In these pages, we're going to find ways to make your stepfamily a success. In fact, we'll make that not only possible, but probable.

Against all odds

We've all heard that about half of the first marriages in the United States end in divorce. Second (and later) marriages fail at an even higher rate—about 60%, according to the Stepfamily Association of America. The rate is higher still when children are part of the package. I don't doubt those statistics, and I'm sure you don't either. Anyone who has attempted to succeed in a marriage that came with a ready-made family knows how incredibly hard it can be.

Among the choices we freely make in this life, deciding to be part of a stepfamily is surely one of the most irrational. And yet we enter into our stepfamilies with such glee! You'd think we'd achieved the fantasy life we dreamed of when we were twelve years old. We wave our hands nonchalantly and roll our eyes, dismissing the dreary statistics. So what if others have failed? We're not like them. So what if stepmoms are stereotyped as "wicked"? We'll shatter that myth with our perfect stepparenting. Former spouses? Our relationships with them will be models for generations to come. Our mistakes of the past are, well, in the past. Only goodness will grace us from now on.

But wait. Something's happened since you walked down the aisle. Things haven't exactly worked out the way you had in mind. Where is the life you planned, and why does the one you're living look so different?

Reality has hit—and hard. Your family-forming plan is a relic of the past. Your schedule has gotten way off track, and your family's progress is falling miserably behind your time line. You feel like you've lost control. Don't worry; you can get it back. You can find the peace you need when you simplify, starting today. You can make choices that will get you and your family moving forward and growing together.

Tales from the Blender

I was totally and blissfully ignorant of how complex, confusing, and strange it would be to become a custodial stepmom to a teen and non-custodial stepmom to a 7 year-old. I never realized I'd be robbed of most of the newly-wed/honeymoon period by having his son in our home, not to mention lots more commotion, chores, and lack of privacy! Quite a culture shock, believe me.

— *Cindy L., Nashville, Tennessee*

My husband and I dated for two years, so I thought I was prepared for taking care of kids. The big difference is that after we were married, I could no longer go home to get away from it. I was living it. Now, when the kids made a mess and tore things up, it was my house and I had to be there to fix it. Now, when I was tired and wanted some peace and quiet and time to myself, I had nowhere to go to find it. It was difficult at first not to feel resentful and selfish.

—*Brenda, Ohio, stepmom of three*

My own childhood was a nightmare. I survived anorexia, I had three stepfathers, and was divorced at twenty-two, following the death of my best friend. But nothing prepared me for the feeling of total lack of control that stepparenting has given me. I feel despair setting in for at least three days before they visit. My weekends used to be lazy affairs with visits to the cinema, restaurants, and beaches, lunch with friends, and drunken nights of fun. Now I spend them babysitting someone else's kids, who wreck my house and make me feel like the wicked woman from the film *Matilda*.

— *Lucinda Green, United Kingdom*

Not Me!

"I can't simplify this mess my life is in," you wail, hands wringing, arms flapping. Yes, you can, if you *choose* to, even though complications will always be there—bickering children, financial concerns, petty ex-spouses, and everything else. Make no mistake about it: you *will* simplify your life, either within your stepfamily or out of it. Here's why: unless you find some peace and simplicity in your life, *you won't have a stepfamily*.

Bringing peace and simplicity into your life doesn't mean that you'll wake up one morning and find that all of your problems have been solved (although that would be a wonderful surprise). Rather, simplifying means coming to terms with the issues your family faces, so that all of you can grow in spite of them.

If you are jealous of the time your husband spends with his kids, you'll have to find a way to reconcile those feelings. If your stepchildren are resisting or rejecting you, you'll have to face that before it overpowers you. These are very real problems, ones that have the potential to destroy your new family. You can't solve all of them by yourself, but you can make progress in the areas that *you can control*. You can understand the limits of your role and not take on things that are someone else's responsibility. This means making the choices that are yours to make, and it can start here and now. So choose simplicity, and defy the oddsmakers.

It won't be easy. In fact, it may be one of the hardest things you've ever done. But if you're prepared and committed, you have a much better chance of success. Make that choice now, and prepare for a long, difficult trek. By taking tiny steps each day, you'll eventually get up that mountain.

If you've ever felt even the ember of a can-do spirit, fan its flames now. By believing in yourself, you'll be able to effect positive change in your stepfamily and simplify your life. Your family will stand a good chance of surviving, even thriving.

What does it mean to choose simplicity?

The simpler life that you're going to create won't look very different on the outside than the life you have now. You'll still have the relationships that complicate your every waking moment, unpleasant commitments and changed plans, conflicting schedules and difficult personalities. Simplicity comes not from your *surroundings*, but from your *approach*.

Choosing simplicity begins and ends in your mind, with believing that you can improve your life one step at a time. Ultimately, it's all about recognizing what you can control—and what you can't control. It's about saying yes to the choices that will bring you fulfillment and peace and saying no to the choices that won't. That's a pretty amazing power.

Let's be very clear about something right up front: You will never have a stepfamily life that's free of complications. *Every* family is complicated. For that matter, life itself is complicated, because there are other people in it with you. Our relationships, and everything that flows from them, enrich our lives—and also complicate them. The trick is to savor the enrichment while reducing the stress.

Choosing simplicity means coming to terms with the everyday struggles in your stepfamily. Some you can eliminate, some you must learn to tolerate, and the rest you can manage on your own terms.

What is it that makes your life seem such a mess? I realize that that must seem like a ridiculous question, but humor me.

Take a moment and make a list of the top five complications in your life. I know that you need more space, but remember, we're simplifying. For now, just think about five of your biggest hassles. We'll come back to this list in a little while.

The biggest complications in my life:

1._____
2._____
3._____
4._____
5._____

Now we have a starting point, but don't get too excited. We have a lot of work to do.

Relinquishing control

Stepmoms suffer from a very strange affliction. It's as if our veins are wide open, allowing everything that happens in our families to shoot straight into our hearts. Then we accept responsibility for all of it, and feel a need to control everyone and everything around us.

I think it's fear of failing that makes us try to control the world. We may feel as if our family began with "failure" stamped on its collective forehead and defeat lurking around every corner. Feeling that way is a terrible disadvantage. It makes us think that if we can just compartmentalize and organize and streamline every detail about everyone in our lives, we'll keep all the bad things away. There will be no more unhappiness or anger or frustration or emptiness in our families because we'll be in charge. It makes sense—but only in our minds.

In the real world, our misguided efforts to control everyone only produce a vicious cycle. When something doesn't turn out as we want, we just try to control more. So, for example, we may try to force a bond with a stepson who isn't ready, because we've decided that's what he needs. When he doesn't respond, we figure we just didn't try hard enough, and push some more. The result is even worse, leaving us frustrated and hurt because we've worked so hard and failed. The disappointment is heavy and draining. Now we're even more afraid of failure in the next issue we take on.

Seeking total control almost guarantees unhappiness. Absolute control isn't possible in *anybody's* life, and especially a stepmom's. You're dealing with a history you may not completely understand and a present that may defy logic. Besides, whether you know it or not, your need to control is taking a toll on you. When you try over and over to control every single situation in your life, you're going to be overwhelmed by the enormous weight on your shoulders—and it doesn't even belong to you.

Are you really that greedy? Put the weight down. Unburden yourself of what isn't yours. Accept the responsibilities that *are* yours. Those should be enough to occupy your time, and they're all you can hope to control anyway. Most importantly, that's where your true security and power lie.

Tales from the Blender

The biggest mistake I made as a stepmom was going overboard. I was so upset that the kids' mom didn't have a bigger part of their lives that I made sure everything was done, that all their projects were lined up. The result was that the kids blamed me when they didn't take responsibility to do their school work or if I knew of a situation that blew up out of control. I became the scapegoat, and felt betrayed and standing alone. The bad part was, I did much of this damage to myself.

— Isabella, New York

I spent a lot of time being angry with my husband's ex-wife and all the anger did was make me feel miserable! It took a long time, but I was finally able to let go and realize that the only person I can control is myself and my reaction to those around me. I learned that you have to let go of thinking you can change or control someone else. You only have power over yourself, and you have the ability to change your reaction to those around you in an attempt to maintain balance in your own life.

—Ann, stepmom of one son

I was getting too involved with all of my stepson's problems and tried too hard to help him, when he didn't want or need me in a parenting role. When I finally detached from the situation, I could concentrate on getting to know him again. I also made his father take a more active role in his son's life. When I stopped nagging about all the bad things my stepson was doing, it helped me become more positive. It hasn't necessarily made me happier, but has given me back a little sanity.

— *Mother of one, stepmom of one*

What do you spend your days trying to control? Earlier, we listed some of the situations that stepmoms and second wives commonly face: juggling the kids' schedules, helping our own parents adjust to their new roles, financial woes, and so on. These can be overwhelming, and it's perfectly natural to want to impose your own order on them. What are you thinking, and what do you do, when you try to take control of these situations?

Think of the things you feel the need to control, manage, or orchestrate *your* way. List five of those things here. Come on—be honest.

I feel the need to control:

1. _____
2. _____
3. _____
4. _____
5. _____

You may feel obligated to take on responsibility for everything related to your stepfamily—again, fearing that if you let go of even one tiny thing, the entire foundation will collapse.

But as you now know, you'll never be able to have complete control. Believe me, I tried—in every possible way, never relenting for a second. But I finally learned that many of my problems resulted not from *lacking* control but from *seeking to impose it* at every turn.

It's a wonder that I didn't alienate my stepsons completely. They were infinitely patient and amazingly tolerant of my attempts to reform them, quickly and completely. Of course, I always told them that I loved them and explained myself with logic, but I was focusing on all the wrong things. Had I controlled *my* reactions more and attempted to control *theirs* less, I would have had more time to laugh and less to cry. I would have lived a simpler, more peaceful life sooner rather than later.

I suspect that a lot of your time and energy, too, are directed toward things that you can't control. Simplifying your life starts with relinquishing some of the control you think you've just got to have.

Look again at your "need to control" list. How often are you able to control everything on it to your satisfaction? How many of those things are truly yours alone to control—and how many involve another person's (or even your entire family's) decisions and choices? How many of these things can you change and improve with *your* time and energy alone?

My point is not that everything is out of your control, but that you must direct your efforts to what is *in* your control—your reactions and your feelings. You are only responsible for how *you* act and feel, and not everyone else. Learn to focus your reactions toward growth for you and your family. Keep it simple, take your time, and make progress, bit by bit. Like the racing tortoise of fairy tale fame, slow and steady is the best plan for stepmoms, too.

Tales from the Blender

I did everything for the kids in the beginning. I washed their clothes, hung them up, fixed snacks, cooked dinner, and even cleaned their rooms for them. I guess I thought that if I did all those things, they would like me and want to live with us. Wrong! I just worked myself to death. They rarely said "thank you" and never a hug or "I love you." Eventually I started losing myself and resenting them. Now I do things when I want to, not to make them want to stay, because I know that doesn't work. I do them because I care.

— *Jenny, mom of one and stepmom of three*

I was childless and eleven years younger than my husband, who had two children from his previous marriage. The kids were crazy about me until they realized that Dad and I were "together" and that it wasn't just them that I was coming to see. I did everything I could to try to reassure them that I was also crazy about them, but it just got worse. That was seven years ago. Slowly, over time, I learned that I didn't have to try so hard to be a parent. You don't get points for how effectively you discipline or pack a box lunch. I learned that the kids needed a friend more than a parent. They already had two who were really good at that job. When I realized this, I started having fun, they started having fun and now we are very happy.

— *Brenda, Alabama, stepmom of two*

What's yours and what's not

Just because you're the stepmom doesn't mean that you must be everyone's keeper. (Do you actually think that's what they *want* you to be?) The mom in you wants to fix everything, smooth the edges, and control the fallout. It sounds reasonable, but it's not. In a stepfamily, and in any family, this simply can't be done and shouldn't be attempted, unless you want to spend the rest of your days in a comfortable room with a garden view and regular visiting hours. You alone cannot repair all that breaks around you. Instead, you need to allow your family to experience growing pains.

Growing pains—yes, they are *painful,* but they also lead to *growth.* They signal that, through trial and error, you're adjusting to each others' personalities and temperaments, agendas and insecurities. Don't be afraid of growing pains. Don't try to intercept them, even when they make you uncomfortable. Instead, learn from them. Don't make it worse by trying to control reactions and events for other family members. Instead, control what is yours.

Take another look at the list of the things you feel the need to control. Now, make a new list. What five things, related to your stepfamily, *do* you have absolute control over? It doesn't matter whether they are big or little, but they must be things entirely within your power that don't need approval or acceptance from anyone else.

For example, on the "need to control" list, you may have written something like "relationship with my stepdaughter." But that is not something you alone can control; you need your stepdaughter's participation and agreement. The corresponding entry on the second list might be: "Stop arguing with my stepdaughter. It takes two, and I can choose not to argue." That's something you *can* control, all by yourself.

Are you starting to recognize the difference between what you *can* control and what you *can't* control? Go ahead; make your list.

Things over which I have complete control:

1. _____
2. _____
3. _____
4. _____
5. _____

Now look all the way back to the very first list you made, the list of complications. Without knowing what you wrote, I'm sure that most of them are things outside of your control. I'm also confident that each one of those items presents choices. Each one has some part you *can* control. Take your time looking at each item, one by one. Think about the choices they offer you, even if several other people are involved. When you simplify your reactions and try to control only what is within your power, you simplify your life.

It's easy to take on far too much as a stepmom and second wife. If you had a hat for every one of your responsibilities, you'd be able to protect the entire population of a small country from sunburn. But taking on the maintenance of everything in your world will only destroy it in the end. And your happiness will be the first casualty.

Finding happiness in a stepfamily isn't always easy. Trying to manufacture happiness is nearly impossible. Relax and simplify. Relieve yourself of the pressure to do the impossible, to control everything that happens in your family. Instead, avail yourself of the opportunity to do the remarkable— to build a family where none existed before.

Growing yourself and your family is not an event. It's a process. You try, you fail, the world doesn't end, and you try again. Every step that guides you toward your family and toward happiness instead of away from it is a good step. Sometimes you'll stumble and will just have to feel your way. But like an infant learning to walk, every stumble means you're trying, reaching out, learning as you go. It's part of the never-ending second chance to make your family work.

Blessed choices

Simplifying your life is about making choices, nothing more. When you understand, down to your soul, that you have the power to make decisions that will simplify your life, you're ready to begin. With a frame of mind based on strength, a belief that you have the power to make your life better, and the courage to make simple choices that are yours to make, you can overcome the odds against you. All you need is a plan and the conviction to carry it out. Make up your mind now that you are going to have the simpler, more positive life that you will choose for yourself and your family.

Being a stepmom means added challenges. Your power to grow your family lies in the choices you make to deal with them. Ignore the challenges and you will be buried in an avalanche of complications. Seize them and you reach the mountaintop. You may be winded and weathered from a few storms, but you'll be victorious nonetheless.

Start with what is right in front of you—where you are and the opportunities that lie before you. After all, you willingly chose the life you are in. Your world may not resemble the one you once planned, but it's *yours*. You wouldn't be here if you didn't love your man beyond reason and believe that the two of you could build a happy life together. Now, make another choice—simply choose to make it better.

Everything you do to promote and enhance your life as a family is a choice. Everything you do to damage and restrict it is a choice. These choices are yours to make.

Choose simplicity. It is the path to growth.

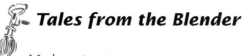 ## *Tales from the Blender*

My happiest moment as a stepmom was one day when my stepdaughter and I were digging in the flower bed. She looked over at me and said, "Ya know what, Jodi? You're a pretty good ol' stepmom." It brought a tear to my eye. I replied that she was a pretty good ol' stepdaughter. There have been numerous occasions that made me proud to be a stepmom, but by far, this one made me the happiest.

— *Jodi Staten, Arkansas*

CHAPTER 2

Simplify Your Expectations

*Go ahead and expect a miracle. Every day
your family grows together and not apart—
that's a miracle.*

I have no doubt that before your marriage, someone told
you what to expect in a stepfamily. It may have been a relative
or a friend; perhaps you read it in a book or saw it on television.
I'm sure that you heard all about the horrors that befall these
relationships. But you probably didn't listen. You were head-
strong and defiant, determined that you would avoid the trauma
others had experienced, because the expectations you had for
your new family were quite logical and thus achievable.

Like many other stepmoms-to-be, you knew just what
your new life would look like: A re-marriage means that people
are moving on with their lives. The past will not interfere.
Former spouses know their places and won't try to corrupt
your new life. Children know all about divorce and
stepfamilies, so they'll take everything in stride. Just in case
they don't, we parents know the warning signs that can mean

trouble. Yes, this family may run into problems, but with a little coaching from you, it will function pretty much like a normal family.

Or so you thought. Then one day you looked around and realized that nothing was as you expected it to be.

"If someone had only told me what to *really* expect in a stepfamily," you may think, "my life sure would be a lot simpler now. I would have had a more realistic plan and a firmer grasp on this unpredictable world I'm living in."

The problem, though, is not the *reality* of your life, but your perception of what it *should* be. You may be expecting the unattainable, some sort of "blended perfection." Or you may be expecting something that really is attainable—a happy, healthy stepfamily—but you're expecting it to happen too quickly. Either way, you've complicated your life with unnecessary pressure and guilt.

Your expectations for your stepfamily need to reflect its unique nature. They must take into account both the delicate relationships that are forming within the family and the very real dangers that lurk beyond it. Your family will never be predictable—*The Brady Bunch* doesn't exist in real life. Your stepfamily won't fit neatly into any preconceived notions, despite your best efforts and intentions. More than anything else, becoming a family is going to require time and patience.

To achieve anything in life, and particularly in your stepfamily, you must have high expectations, but they must also be reasonable ones. A stepmom has more than enough to worry about without creating more worries all by herself. In this chapter, you'll learn to examine the expectations you have now and the ones you'll continue to form. You'll learn how to let go of unrealistic expectations and enjoy the simplicity and growth that follow.

You may feel that you've already given up more in your family life than you had available to begin with, but trust me here. You need to give up a few more things—the unrealistic expectations that are complicating your life to no end. When you expect too much from yourself and the rest of your family, you complicate an already difficult situation. You put pressure on yourself to meet your expectations right away, when the process of building your family will take years. It's just like everyone told you, back when you weren't ready to listen. Listen now.

A stepfamily is a brand-new being, a Frankenstein of sorts, that has to learn to grow on its own. You may plan for it and study it and even dissect it, but you can't develop it in a vacuum. You have to work around the gazillion other people problems that creep into your brilliantly-laid plans. So inject a little realism into your expectations. If you don't, the monster may destroy you.

When I first became a stepmother, I expected my relationship with my stepsons to make others stand in awe and amazement. Since the boys seemed to accept me fully, even before the marriage, this made sense at the time. I not only expected it, I couldn't see any reason that it couldn't happen, exactly as I wanted—and instantly, too!

My stepsons were loving and welcoming, but that wasn't enough for me. I expected them to love me the same way my own son did. I thought every moment that wasn't Norman

Rockwell-perfect was cause for concern. If they didn't hug me as spontaneously or as often as they hugged their dad, I thought they didn't really love me. I failed to notice that they always accepted *my* hugs. I was so preoccupied with the bigger picture that I didn't recognize that little miracle.

When my plan to create the world's best stepmom-stepchild relationship didn't materialize on my tight schedule, I blamed myself and tried even harder. But that only frustrated me more, as I searched for results that never came quickly or consistently enough. My disappointment was palpable. I was trying so hard to meet my expectation that I couldn't see that I was, in fact, getting where I wanted to go.

The subtle changes that signaled a deepening relationship didn't come about because of anything I did, but simply because the time we spent together brought us closer. This relationship could not be rushed. My heart was in the right place, but my expectation was unreasonable, as were my efforts and my timetable. Had I not expected so much so fast, I could have enjoyed the journey a little more. My relationship with my stepsons happened at a slower rate, but it was my own simple miracle just the same.

I came to my marriage with other expectations, too, and it hurt when they didn't materialize. I was afraid of my husband's ex-wife, uncomfortable around his family, and overwhelmed by the increased work of having two more kids in the house. I also was running interference between my husband and my son, and my husband and my ex-husband. All of that was unnecessary, but I didn't know it.

I also expected my husband to understand what I was going through. I thought he would see how hard everything was for me, but he didn't. That worried me even more. I couldn't even talk about some of it. I could barely admit to myself how I felt, because I didn't expect to feel that way (how ironic is that?). I now can see that the reason my husband didn't "get it" was that I had manufactured a lot of the turmoil myself. But it all felt very real to me, and it hurt when he didn't understand. I couldn't believe he was that uncaring; he couldn't believe I was that paranoid.

What expectations do you have for your marriage and stepfamily? Even if you've never said them out loud or written them down, they are nonetheless very real and you know what they are. Write down a few of the expectations you have for your stepfamily. Soon you'll be able to see whether they are reasonable and achievable or if they are merely added complications that you can do without.

My expectations for my stepfamily:

1._____
2._____
3._____

Tales from the Blender

Being a stepmom is nothing like I expected. When I first met my husband's children, they were so sweet and they seemed to like me. I thought, "I can do this." I must have been delusional.

Two weeks after we got married I found myself in a war. We ended up going to court to get custody of his three children. It was the hardest, most painful thing I had ever done. We were analyzed to see if we would be fit parents. We had to take psychological tests to see if we were mentally stable. But I still wanted to be a stepmom to these kids.

That was only the beginning of a long and stressful four years. More summers in court fighting over the children. Kids saying "I hate you" and "You're not my mother." Social workers showing up on our doorstep because the "ex" had reported us for neglect or physical abuse. The children even started lying, reporting us for things we could have never done. There were some good times. But the bad seemed to overshadow the good.

I also thought I would have a decent relationship with the bio mom. Wrong!!! She was rude on the phone when she called to talk to the kids. And she wasn't paying any child support, which just made me resent her more.

Only one child lives with us now, and our relationship is good. But it is still hard. Sometimes I get a huge knot in my stomach wondering what his "ex" will do next. It never ends.

— *Jenny, mom of one and stepmom of three*

Give up unrealistic expectations

Your unique circumstances will determine the expectations that you have for your family. Still, there are three flawed expectations that almost every stepmom-to-be has when she says "I do." These need to be purged from your system like corrupted computer files and replaced with new ones that will run a lot more smoothly.

Let's examine these faulty expectations one by one. Grab a cup of coffee; this may take a while.

Unrealistic Expectation No. 1: *I'll know how to be a good stepmom because I already am a good mom (or aunt or babysitter or whatever).*

Reality: *No, you won't, not right away, but you can learn.*

This expectation appears to make a lot of sense. Kids are kids, right? You can say, "brush your teeth" to four kids as easily as you can to two, so what's the problem? You'll just treat your stepchildren the same way you treat your children, and you'll be loved and embraced equally by all the little people in your life.

If it's so logical, why does it complicate your life so? Part of it is has to do with the kids. Stepchildren are often mourning the family they have lost, and bring that grief into their new family. Besides, they don't know how to be stepkids any more than you know how to be a stepmom. Their roles, like yours, are as clear as stumpwater. So ease up on yourself and everyone else. Give yourself time to adjust to the new role you're playing. Stepmothering is not innate.

🥄 *Tales from the Blender*

There are times when I think being a stepmom is harder than being a bio-mom, because I am in a role where I am expected to do all the mom things, yet have little control and no right to expect affection or loyalty from these kids.

— *Polly Bywater, Tulsa, Oklahoma, mom of four, stepmom of five, custodial of two*

Many new stepmoms feel they need to quickly fill any void in the child's life. If the child pulls away and rejects you, you may feel that you've failed, and fear that you'll never build the bond you want with your stepchild. But that isn't necessarily so. Some things that have worked before may not work with your stepchildren, just because they are different individuals. Finding that a tried and true approach doesn't work can be extremely stressful and frustrating. But it isn't failure; it's practice. And there's no way around it.

Becoming a stepmother is an excellent cure for a bad memory, because you will remember every cross word or hurt feeling between you and your stepchild. It's a guarantee. So make those memories worth something. Each time you examine the hurts to find the lessons that are buried within, you come one step closer to meeting your expectation. Day by day, you're becoming a better stepmother.

I learned fairly quickly, though not painlessly, that my stepsons were different from my son in certain ways. Neither way was right or better; I just had to learn that I couldn't expect the same results with the same approach every time. I finally figured out that it wasn't control of the kids that I lacked, but control of *myself*. I realized that I could be a good stepmom and get results by using what worked. I just needed time to find out what that was. So do you.

Tales from the Blender

My attempts to gain my 7 year-old stepson's favor often disappoint me, because I'm still trying to figure out his likes and dislikes and understand his point of view, which never ceases to baffle and bewilder me. When I made spaghetti, his favorite food, he burst into tears, because he hadn't told me that he hates sauce of any kind. I thought an Easter egg hunt would be a fun activity for us all to enjoy together. As it turned out, he dislikes them because they're too competitive, and then, when he didn't find as many eggs as other kids did, he ended up angry and frustrated.

After failing to please him one too many times, I decided I would be less stressed out and feel more in control if I stopped trying so hard to please him and accept that I'm responsible only for my own happiness. I still brainstorm ways I can connect with him, but I no longer try to anticipate his reactions or let myself have expectations about how long it will take for us to bond or try to measure how close we are.

Our relationship will develop as it is meant to develop, and not a second sooner. I can do things to encourage it to bloom, but more important than any action I can take, I can be patient, tolerant, and flexible. I can choose not to take his indifference personally and not to take for granted the little moments that make my heart smile, like the hug we shared when the two of us as a team beat his dad at a board game. The small successes that move us a tiny bit closer to the ultimate goal have become my focus, and I'm much more at peace because of that choice.

— S.S., *Colorado*

Simplify your life by trading the "kids are kids" expectation for a more realistic one: *I expect that I will have to learn how to be a good stepmom, and I can get there with time and patience.*

Stepmothering is a precarious job. It's like walking through a minefield carrying an armful of bowling balls. With each step, you're likely to detonate a bomb. Simplify your days by relieving yourself of the expectation that you'll be a good stepmom the instant your name is etched on the mailbox. Accept that you will make mistakes. (I think some of mine have been enshrined in the Screw-Up Hall of Fame.) The mistakes will lead you toward your goal, if you let them.

By revising your expectation about your relationship with your stepchildren, you acknowledge that becoming a stepmom is a learning experience, not a skill you've tucked away, just waiting to use. It won't be automatic just because you think it should be. When you relieve yourself of the expectation that you will become the kind of stepmom you envision overnight, you give yourself some much-needed breathing room.

Accepting that you will *learn* how to be the stepmom your stepkids need allows for repeated attempts, failures, and re-plays—in other words, the chance to keep going. Put your energies into learning as you go. Don't expect to know it all at the beginning—or ever, for that matter. Learning how to be a stepmom is a process, not an event.

By expecting to make *progress*, rather than achieve *perfection*, you'll be able to handle the setbacks more easily. Each time your relationship feels unsatisfying or incomplete is a signal that you can learn something from the situation. When you know what doesn't work, you can discover what *does* by having the courage to try again—to risk making another mistake, because the rewards of success are so great.

When I finally was able to choose progress over perfection, my mistakes didn't seem so bad. It was as if each had come with a warning: "Use for instructional purposes only." You can approach your mistakes the same way. You can languish in them—or learn from them. There's even a hidden bonus, a way to make good use of all the pressure you've been putting on yourself: Pressure yourself to learn from your mistakes. That will get you closer to where you want to be.

When you do become a good stepmom (and you may even become a *great* stepmom), it will be because you worked toward it every day, because you allowed yourself to stumble in a role that comes with far more questions than answers, because you learned from those mistakes, and because you gave yourself the time and opportunities to reach your goal. That will be quite an accomplishment.

When you approach stepmothering with the right frame of mind—accepting that there will be trial and error, gain and loss—you allow yourself to manage it, instead of it managing you and destroying your family in the process. Becoming a good stepmom is part intuition and part luck, but mostly perseverance. You can learn how to do it your own way, one day at a time. You can become a capable, compassionate, and caring stepmom. That's what your stepchildren need, and that's enough. That's what is reasonable to expect of yourself. It's worth the work and the wait.

Tales from the Blender

I knew and got along with my stepson and his mother before I knew his father, so when our relationship began to get serious, I honestly didn't think that becoming a stepmother to his child would be as complicated as it has turned out to be. Over the years, I have matured enough to understand that true love takes work on both sides. I've also learned that the bond you create with your stepchild is not as easily obtained as that with your biological children. By stepping back a bit and becoming more of a guiding figure in his life rather than trying to be a mother figure, we all seem to get along better. Without the expectations, I no longer feel rejected by my stepson and I can handle his mother's actions better.

— Kim Peterson, mom of two & stepmom of one

From the beginning, I told my stepkids that I was not competing with their mom. That I loved their father and wanted to be there to watch them grow into adults. I said that I would never come between them and their parents. Slowly introduce yourself in their lives. Its a big change for everyone and it won't happen overnight.

— Isabella, New York

Unrealistic Expectation No. 2: *This marriage will be easier than the one(s) before it.*

Reality: *It may be easier in some ways, but the strains of being in a stepfamily will test your marriage every day.*

Whether or not you've been married before, you probably know what a bad relationship feels like and you don't want to go through that again. Besides, you're so much in love with your man that you can't see straight. So what's the problem? It's really quite simple: any marriage is complicated, and yours is super-complicated. For goodness sake, don't complicate it any more by expecting it to survive without having to fight for it.

In many, many ways, this will be a much harder marriage. As in any relationship, there are going to be tiny aggravations as well as major conflicts with your spouse—who is, after all, an independent being and not your clone. Besides that, you have the added task of dealing with the strains that your husband's children, your children (if you have them), and former spouses put on your marriage. This marriage will be harder because of the added weight of many things that you cannot control.

Now that I've gotten you sufficiently depressed, here's the good news: your marriage also has strengths that will help it survive, if you refocus your expectation and keep it simple. We'll take a look at those in just a bit.

Trade in unrealistic expectations about your marriage for this one: *I expect to have a wonderful, strong marriage, but I also expect there to be difficulties surrounding us that we will overcome together.*

With this expectation, you're a grown-up who understands that no marriage is a bed of roses all the time. Keep that in focus, and don't forget that this marriage needs even more of your protection and nurturing than your previous one(s) did. Expecting there not to be any bumps along the way only gives more power to them when they do occur, as they will in every marriage.

This is going to be a more difficult marriage. That much you can count on. But it can be a much stronger marriage, too. The catch is that you'll have to fight for it. Expect that, too. Understand and accept the uphill battle your marriage faces, in an environment that won't always be friendly.

A few years into our marriage, I told my husband that I completely understood why more second marriages fail than first marriages do. The state of constant change and unpredictability in our home scared me to death. My struggles with the kids and my struggle to control every moment of our lives was putting a terrible strain on us. I was so very insecure that every minor irritation became a major threat. I felt overwhelming stress at times, and I was stunned by the ways our marriage had suffered. I wanted my marriage to feel safe and secure, but instead I often felt weak and vulnerable. If I could feel such distance from my husband, I thought, something must be terribly wrong.

At times, my marriage was far, far from what I had expected. I cried a lot. But I love my husband more than the air I breathe, and I knew that we could have the kind of life together that we both want. I knew it had to simpler than I was making it. I had to learn that there indeed would be problems, even in a marriage as strong and as meant-to-be as I believe ours is. Revising my expectation helped simplify my worries and reduce complications to just that—issues that we could resolve, not threats to our marriage.

Tales from the Blender

I've seen too many marriages destroyed because the couple was not able to handle the complex issues of a stepfamily, such as children trying to turn the parents against each other, lack of communication between family members or one feeling unable to communicate with the others, interference from extended family members or the birth parent, or a spouse not standing by their partner and letting their feelings become second to the children's wishes and desires. Be honest with yourself: can you really handle these issues? Because if you can't, it can destroy your marriage.

— *Kim Peterson, mom of two & stepmom of one*

Stepfamily issues don't have to become threats to your marriage, because you also bring important strengths to it. Let's look at those strengths now.

1. Perhaps your greatest strength is your ***determination to succeed***. You've formed a stepfamily because something else failed. Since you don't want that to happen again, your instinct for survival kicks in and perseverance follows. Your desire and drive to make this marriage work will sustain you through tough times. Stepmoms don't give up easily. The will to keep going is a great strength.

2. While you're fighting so hard for your marriage, you'll repeatedly draw on your ***creativity***. Dealing with a non-traditional family situation often requires unconventional thinking. A willingness to try new solutions is a great strength. Don't be afraid to look for unusual answers and to try some uncommon approaches. Your and your husband's ingenuity will surface, and your marriage will benefit. Trust your instincts. What's right is what works for *your* marriage.

3. We'd all like to live our lives without problems or pain. But significant life experiences, even the painful ones, are never wasted. Having survived everything that preceded your marriage, you and your husband bring to it a ***maturity*** that will strengthen you. Judge less, compromise more. Find a new perspective. Draw on everything you've learned and use the skills that experience has given you. Keep an eye on the big picture. The survival of your marriage is far more important than any immediate crisis you face. Your hard-won maturity makes that very clear.

All of these strengths, as well as others you'll uncover, make you and your husband a formidable team. Facing those difficult problems *together* is what it's all about. Expect there to be problems—but expect also that, working as a team, you will resolve them.

Unrealistic Expectation No. 3: *My family will not take as long to "blend" as other stepfamilies.*
Reality: *Yes, it will—and possibly longer. But that's okay.*

It's quite normal to long for instantaneous peace and serenity, family bonding, and a picturesque home life. When that doesn't happen, you may forget what an enormous challenge stepfamily life is, and may only be able to see that your family isn't "there" yet. It's a terribly destructive expectation.

It's understandable to want to skip the early period of hardship and frustration and get right to the years of being the kind of family you want to become. After the turmoil and sadness that often precede re-marriage, we want things to be calm and settled. We often are unprepared for the new complications that replace the ones we've just left behind. But we only add to our stress by expecting too much from our family members—and especially ourselves—way too soon.

There is something unbelievably hard about creating one family out of two. I heard the same prediction that you probably did—that it can take as long as *eight years* for a "family" to emerge from the hodgepodge of personalities that are thrust together in a stepfamily. I ignored the advice and expected more, sooner. I was wrong.

My stepfamily began under fortunate circumstances. Our sons truly enjoyed each other's company and the adults usually behaved like adults. I thought that a stepfamily like ours, free of squabbling children and serious legal problems, would be able to fast-forward through the time supposedly required for "blending." I thought that deep feelings of connection would arrive at our new home about the same time as the first phone bill. I thought we might even start to look like each other after a while.

So I wasn't prepared for the disjointed feelings that I sometimes had. I was sorely disappointed when, after several months, even good months, there still were times that I felt I was an actor in a play, that my life was surreal, that I had been crazy to imagine we could ever be a real family. Sometimes, when I watched my husband and my stepsons, I sensed a deep sadness in them. Although the boys spent about half their time with us, I was afraid it wasn't enough. I often felt that *I* should be the one who left on Sunday evenings.

I thought we'd never overcome the grief we'd all experienced. A few times, I had the heartbreaking sensation that we were just kidding ourselves. We were sharing a house, but not a life. Trying to build something new was not only too hard—maybe it was even wrong.

A therapist probably would have looked at our family and said that we were doing fairly well and had a good prognosis for success. But that wouldn't have been enough for me. I thought that if I only worked hard enough, my stepfamily would have a lightning-fast adjustment and sky-high level of satisfaction.

I finally learned that those who insist that new stepfamilies need time to adjust are called "experts" for a good reason. I didn't understand then that only time, not more effort on my part, could make the painful feelings go away. Expecting to become an instant family caused me to take setbacks harder than I should have, only because I had refused to believe that they actually might occur.

Throw away any unrealistic expectation you have about the time your family will need to grow together. Replace it with a better one: *I expect that my family will grow and become whole, but I also expect that it will take an indefinite amount of time, and I am willing to be patient.*

There, isn't that better? You have the same basic expectation, but you no longer have the added pressure of a deadline. You have the same admirable goal, but you've simplified your days by acknowledging that a well-adjusted, growing family isn't right around the corner. When setbacks occur—and they will—they won't destroy your expectation, because they now are *part of* your expectation. Reversals are manageable when you learn from what goes right and what goes wrong. Setbacks become merely teaching tools, not the end of your family.

There is great hope and power in greeting every day with "we're still learning, but we're making progress." Giving yourself permission to be like other stepfamilies—families that need time to adapt and adjust—is one of the greatest gifts you can give yourself. Then you can concentrate on taking the steps needed to become a "real family" (whatever you consider that to be), one day at a time, learning as you go. Take however much time your family needs. It's not a race; it's about reaching your personal best.

Tales from the Blender

My husband and I *both* had the misconception that it wouldn't take our family as long to "blend" as the experts told us it would. We're intelligent, compassionate people and we love each other and each other's children very much. We each were divorced for several years prior to finding each other and thought we'd had enough time to work through all our issues and mistakes of the past and had "gotten it right" this time. The thing we overlooked, however, is that in being on our own for so many years, we each developed our own way of doing things.

For example, we each had (and continue to have) very different expectations of the kids and their roles in the household. As a single mom for nearly seven years, I learned that in order to maintain my sanity, I had to concentrate my energies on the most important things and let others slide. I opted to spend quality time with my kids and not worry about keeping my house immaculate. My husband, on the other hand, was basically a bachelor for eight years. His home was always neat and orderly. His *life* was neat and orderly. But I think we can all agree that stepfamily life is *not* neat and orderly.

He and I are now raising three children together, all of whom are either teenagers or pre-teenagers. They're coming from a place in which the expectations of them were different than they are in this new household.

Our daily life is a constant struggle to compromise our expectations so that we can all peacefully co-exist.

—*Debbie Budesky, Marshall, Michigan*

Meeting others' expectations

Besides carrying your own expectations on your tired shoulders, you probably have also loaded on the ones that you imagine others have for you. There are many people whose family lives intersect with that of your stepfamily—former spouses, their new spouses, your children's other stepsiblings, and so on. You may feel as if you are continually adjusting to their schedules and their needs. Because of that, you may spend way too much time worrying about what someone else expects you to do.

You may think that if you don't work wonders in every aspect of your new life, other people will be ready to judge you and dispense punishment. You can't have a "normal" life with "normal" troubles because everyone expects you to succeed, instantly, and they're ready to give you a swift kick in the psyche if you blunder. You can't allow yourself to fall short of perfection because this is what you wanted, darn it, and you had better enjoy it!

Well, excuse me, but, *says who?*

When you feel obligated to meet other people's expectations—whether real or imagined—you complicate your life. Those kinds of "obligations" have to go, and don't let the screen door hit them in their backside, as my grandmother used to say. Basing your family life on the expectations of others doesn't help you reach your goals. In fact, it will only confuse you as you work to simplify the choices you have to make. (We'll talk much more about obligations and goals in the next chapter.)

This expectation is so easy to simplify that it makes me want to say a big "thank you" to the gods of all stepmoms (in spite of the not-so-great things they also send our way). This one is truly a no-brainer. Read it, remember it, tape it to your mirror if you need to:

❖ What others may want is irrelevant and out of your control. Don't worry about what others expect, whether that expectation is real or exists only in your imagination.

❖ What others may think of you or expect from you is not important unless you make it so. Don't waste your time trying to understand others' expectations, and don't feel obligated to explain your choices.

Your energy and resources will be taxed just working to meet the goals that you have set for yourself and your family. Other people's expectations can become a tremendous burden that you can do without. So choose your expectations wisely.

No one but you knows what you are going through each day. Other stepmoms can understand and commiserate, but only *you* have to deal with the complications of your life. What I expect or what your mother expects or what your ex-husband expects is irrelevant. All that matters is what *you* expect. Keep your expectations realistic and reachable, and give yourself enough time to meet your expectations. Focus on *your* choices and *your* goals, and no one else's.

I know that there are people in your life who have your best interests at heart, and you probably respect them and value their opinions. From time to time, they may explicitly tell you what they expect of you. That's fine; that's their prerogative. But you still have a choice—to make their expectations part of your own or to reject them. Ask yourself whether their expectation dovetails with what you want. Will meeting *their* expectation bring *you* more happiness? Will meeting *their* expectation help you achieve *your* goal? You are the one who decides what goals to pursue. It's your choice to make.

Your path to happiness and a healthy family is paved with the progress you make toward your goals each day. Aren't your own expectations, even realistic ones, enough to keep you busy? Yours are the only expectations that matter. Simplify your expectations for your life—real or imagined, yours or someone else's—by taking a tip from the Cub Scouts: Do your best. That's all. That's manageable. That's simple.

Savor the small victories

Expectations, even reasonable ones, sometimes are not met. When that happens, we may feel disappointment or pain. But sometimes we try so hard to meet expectations, realistic or otherwise, that we blind ourselves to progress that is right there before us. When, on the other hand, we lower our expectations and raise our awareness, we're often blessed with wonderful surprises. Don't miss those tiny miracles when they happen.

Maybe you're not the world's greatest stepmom (yet), but that spontaneous hug from your stepson shows that you're headed in the right direction. Focus on milestones like that, rather than the events that left you feeling like a candidate for the world's *worst* stepmom. Look for the encouraging moments that mean you're getting somewhere. One moment at a time, remembered and cherished, is what builds a great relationship.

Be on the lookout for the wonderful things going on at your house. A few years ago, I discovered something wonderful at mine.

Every once in a while, my stepsons couldn't come for one of their regular visits because of some scheduling conflict. My son never failed to ask if something else could be worked out. If only one of the boys had another commitment, could the other stepbrother come? If the problem was that my husband wasn't available to drive them, could their mom bring them over? It was happening the other way as well. If my son wasn't here when my stepsons came over, their first question was, "When's he coming home?" They'd ask again and again, countless times, until he arrived.

These questions may seem trivial, but once I'd thought about it I realized that they were a sign that our families were becoming more one than two. It was one of those small steps that I finally could appreciate.

As you build your family, be sure that you take the time to recognize the growth along the way. Don't ignore the small gains when they happen, and then don't forget them. Be aware of every bit of progress you make, for that is what will sustain you. These bright moments sometimes will surprise you, if you'll just take the time to notice.

A stepmom's path is long and is often a struggle. Keep things in perspective and be aware of the process. Don't work so hard for perfection that you miss the baby steps you've taken along the way. Little by little, those tiny steps will help you realize your goals.

Return to the list of expectations you made at the beginning of this chapter. Are they reasonable and within your control? Can you see the choices they present, and the ways you can achieve them? Do they fill you with encouragement and hope for your family? If not, revise them so that they do, using what you've learned.

If your expectations are realistic and reachable, they will guide you toward your goals. Make them tools that help, not burdens that disappoint. Re-evaluate your expectations, and do the best that you can for yourself and your family today. Then do it again tomorrow. Do it with the time and patience that's needed to transform strangers into kin.

You alone can decide what expectations to have for yourself and your family. These, in turn, will go a long way toward guiding your behavior. Progress at the pace that's right for you. Expect to succeed, but simplify the path to success by keeping your expectations reasonable and finding what works. Adjust as you go—not because you've failed, but because you're always learning a better way. Realize that building a stepfamily is a massive but rewarding challenge, and expect to give your best to achieve it.

Make your own miracles.

Tales from the Blender

Although my three stepdaughters basically forgot me on Mothers Day, they more than made up for it a few weeks later when I had food poisoning and spent an entire day on the couch or in the bathroom. The girls all felt so bad for me. The youngest gave me her favorite blanket and stuffed animal to lie with. The middle child poured me 7-Up and juice all day and made sure my blanket was tucked in really well so I wouldn't be cold. The oldest made chicken soup and served it to me. They were all extra kind and considerate. They even checked on me by phone from their mom's house the next day. The cutest thing was that all three of them kissed my belly (I am pregnant) to make sure the baby would be okay.

It doesn't get any better than this.

— *Kathi O., stepmom and mom-to-be*

CHAPTER 3

Simplify Your Obligations, Set Your Goals

The simplest path is a straight line.

Because a stepmom's life is full yet unfamiliar, it's easy to feel overpowered by obligations, whether real or imagined. In your efforts to *do* all and *be* all, you may use a shotgun approach. Since you're unclear about where to direct your efforts, you aim at everything in sight.

There is enough real work to do as a stepmom without adding to it needlessly. You simplify your life when you have the *clarity* to identify your real targets and eliminate the rest. Clarity is indispensable. It allows you to maintain the *focus* you need to build the best life you can for yourself and your family. Simply put, when you are clear about what you *have* to do (your obligations), you can focus on what you *want* to do (your goals). Healthy doses of both clarity and focus will enhance everything you do, help you to grow each day, and lead you to the peace and serenity that you crave.

If this sounds powerful, that's because it is. And you won't need to move to Siberia, inhale tranquilizers, or wait until the kids are grown to reap the benefits.

It all starts with identifying and understanding your obligations. They're not as bad as you think—really! The obligations you have as a stepmom require a commitment, but they don't need to keep you from reaching goals that are important to you. As with everything else, you have a great deal of control and many choices.

Understanding your obligations

In entering your stepfamily, you took on several obligations, and there is no question that they affect the range of choices you have. For instance, do you have a *choice* about respecting your stepchildren's other family? No, that's an *obligation* that came with your marriage. Does that mean you have an *obligation* to be bosom buddies with your stepchildren's mom? No, you have a *choice* about the quality of your relationship with her.

Accept the responsibilities that come with your obligations. They don't mean the end of your free will; they're just a part of who you are now. If you had not married your husband, you probably wouldn't have these other people in your life, but because you made that decision, you have obligations to them.

Don't fight your obligations. Instead, honor them with grace and simplicity. If you want to be best friends with your stepchildren's mom, that's fine (though some would call it suicidal!), but your obligation to her ends with respect. Any effort you make to complicate your life beyond that is your own choice.

Before we go any further, make a list of what you feel are your top five obligations as a stepmom and second wife.

I feel obligated to:

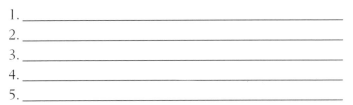

1. _____
2. _____
3. _____
4. _____
5. _____

Now, let's see if we can simplify any of these. Remember, we're looking for the control and choices that you have. They really do exist, amid your obligations.

Different kinds of obligations

As you think about your obligations as a stepmom, you'll discover that they fall into one of two categories, each presenting its own set of options. There are the *life-imposed* obligations that result from decisions we've made—the big ones, like marrying a man with children, or having children of our own. But many of the obligations we worry ourselves about are actually *self-imposed* ones that we can change if we wish. What we may think of as an *exterior obligation* (a life-imposed one) may actually be an *internal choice* (a self-imposed one) that we have made all by ourselves to complicate our lives. For example, are you obligated to remind your husband to pay his child support? No; it's not your responsibility. But if you believe it's up to you to keep track of it (maybe even writing the check for him, muttering under your breath as you do), that's a *choice* you've made.

To simplify your messy life, eliminate the self-imposed obligations that you don't want or need. Your control comes in how you choose to respond to your obligations and what you choose to do to fulfill them.

Many situations present opportunities to make your life either more simple or more complex. Returning to a previous example, you have the life-imposed obligation to respect your stepchildren's mom. Believe it or not, this provides you with options. You can choose the simple route and honor her place in the children's lives. Or you can take a more complicated route and get overly involved in her life. Which sounds better to you?

Any "obligations" that result from taking the more complicated route are completely self-imposed. These are the ones that you can choose to keep or eliminate. They are entirely at your discretion. Even if you decide to keep them, control over subsequent choices still is yours.

Do you understand the difference between the obligations and choices in your life? As we've discussed, you have a life-imposed obligation to be civil and fair to all the former spouses in your life. An "obligation" to celebrate every holiday together is self-imposed, possibly masochistic, and entirely optional. How does that simplify your life?

You have a life-imposed obligation to parent your step-children the best you can. An "obligation" to grant them special privileges or excuse them from rules of your home is self-imposed, counterproductive, and entirely optional. How does that simplify your life?

You have a life-imposed obligation to parent your own children the best you can. An "obligation" to grant them their every wish while ignoring your own interests is self-imposed, unhealthy, and entirely optional. How does that simplify your life?

You have a life-imposed obligation to strengthen your marriage and support your husband. An "obligation" to protect him from his ex-wife or assume full responsibility for his children is self-imposed, damaging, and entirely optional. How does that simplify your life?

These are examples of some basic life-imposed obligations that many of us deal with by virtue of our marriages. Accept that they exist, then alter them to fit your life. The self-imposed obligations are the ones that are optional. You and you alone have the ability to accept or reject them. They are yours to control.

Of course, there may be times when you willingly take on a self-imposed obligation. For example, you do not have the obligation to care for your husband's children alone, just because he or their mom asks. But if you decide to accept that responsibility, you have an obligation to do it well. You've obligated yourself by agreeing to the request. And there's nothing wrong with doing that—a self-imposed obligation isn't *always* bad! But it *is* always your choice.

There probably are very few life-imposed obligations for which you have full responsibility. Make no mistake—they are big obligations, but you have the ability to manage them. Everything you do to fulfill those obligations is your choice to make. You can choose the simple or the complicated route. Everything you do that is unrelated to an obligation is another choice. Recognizing that simple fact simplifies your life.

Review the list you made a few moments ago. Add to it if you've thought of something new. Now give each one a hard look. Are all of these truly *life*-imposed obligations? Which are actually *choices* that you've made and that you can eliminate? Identifying and labeling them is the first step in simplifying them.

Even in our messy lives as stepmoms, we have enormous power over our lives on a daily basis. And if we can get through today without need of a therapist or lawyer, we'll have a better shot at tomorrow and all the days after that.

Tales from the Blender

My stepdaughter's mother would sacrifice anything, including her child, to be with her boyfriend. I became very resentful of mothering her child while she escaped her responsibilities as a mother. I love my stepdaughter and feel horrible for her, but I have a life and a marriage as well! My husband and I made the decision not to enable this woman to not be a mother. We do not take my stepdaughter whenever her mother feels like going out. We have set boundaries. It was hard for my husband because he would rather take her, but how else will the "ex" ever learn that we are not babysitters?

— *Michele, stepmom of one*

Dealing with my husband's ex-wife destroyed our lives. I did it to keep the peace, because he either would fight with her or agree to anything, just to get her off the phone. So I took over and things went smoothly. However, every time the two of them talked, it all fell apart. The end result was frustration and anger, and he never learned how to deal with her like an adult. I have since married again and this time I don't manage the ex-wife for my husband. I do talk to her, but only when necessary. It is his problem.

— *Kathi O., stepmom and mom-to-be*

Establishing your goals

Once you achieve clarity in understanding your obligations—what you *have* to do—then you can focus on what you *want* to do. That's where you'll find tremendous freedom, opportunity, and happiness. That's where you'll find your *goals*.

Your goals are like your heartbeat. They will keep you going in the face of difficult obligations in your life. They will define you and sustain you. Because they reflect what is in your heart, they deserve your time and attention.

It's possible that you haven't taken the time to set goals since becoming a stepmom. You're focused on just getting through the day, and there are times when that alone can be quite an achievement! But you also need to have long-term goals that promote your health and that of your family. Without them, your life is complicated by indecision and confusion. You can't move forward. Without goals, you have no purpose.

You may feel that setting goals and reaching them will take up too much of your limited time. Actually, the opposite is true. Your goals will protect your valuable time because they give you *focus*, something that is easily misplaced in a blended (shaken, stirred, and pulverized) family. The focus on clear goals will simplify everything that follows.

A stepmom's failure to reach, or even set, goals comes not from lack of ability or opportunity, but from allowing unimportant things to get in the way. We put ourselves under so much pressure to conquer all that lies in our wake (that shotgun approach again) that we spend our energy in insignificant, non-productive, even destructive ways, because we don't know what we really need or want to do. We tread water instead of swimming ashore.

We think that we need to micromanage every detail of our lives. Somebody has to tend to this mess, by golly, and it looks like we're elected. We give everything equal importance only to realize, six months down the road, that nothing has changed. Our "just-get-me-through-this-crisis" mentality has blocked our view of the horizon. We haven't gotten anywhere in the grand scheme of our lives—we've just been fighting fires, with no thought of the final outcome.

Without a clear focus on what we're doing, we have no priorities, no plan, no guidance. Without focus, we have a tendency to do the wrong things. Without focus, there can be no growth. We're left without progress or accomplishment, just feelings of inadequacy, regret, and confusion. That is what happens when we're not working toward a goal.

So what are your goals? Right now, if someone asked you what you wanted in life, you'd probably say, "Just give me maid. That would at least simplify *something*." You'd be right, but that wouldn't get you closer to achieving your life goals. The answers to two very simple yet critical questions will bring relief from the chaos you see today. In time, they will bring you tremendous growth.

To find the focus you need for a simpler life and to be able to set goals for achieving it, spend a while thinking about these two questions as they relate to your role as stepmom:

> *What do you want?*
> *Does this choice get you closer to your goal?*

Your answers to the first question will give you focus. Your answers to the second will help you make the choices you must make on a daily basis. They are completely within your power and control.

What do you want?

Do you know what you want from your roles as stepmom and wife? It's the most important question you have to answer, because your answers will determine everything that follows.

The answers must come from your heart and soul. They must reflect *your* goals alone. Establish great goals for your life and you'll have the focus that will enable you to achieve them. Once you know your goals, the clutter will disappear, your choices will become clearer, and you will have a simpler life.

I have few rules about goals, but one is that they must be positive. Goals such as "get the kids out of the house" or "make my ex-husband's life miserable" don't qualify. In fact, they are self-destructive. You can't grow when you're focused on the negative. You can't simplify when you spend your energy on unproductive, time-consuming, mean-spirited activities.

It's also best to answer *what do you want?* with responses that don't have a beginning or end. Each day brings so many new challenges that we can easily feel trapped by deadlines or unreachable expectations. But if we set goals that are *pro-*

cesses rather than *products*, we allow for the inevitable setbacks that populate our lives. Our control comes by making progress toward our goals. If each day you can get nearer to where you want to be, you'll continue to grow, enjoying more peace and serenity along the way.

The goals you set will determine how you spend much of your time and energy. That's why your goals need to be about *you* and what *you* can control. "Having a perfect stepfamily" is not something over which you have complete control (not to mention that it's a goal you'll never achieve). "Being a patient, loving stepmom," on the other hand, is a goal that you can set for yourself and work toward by yourself. It is a goal that you can get closer to every day through the choices that you make. Achieving that goal certainly will improve and simplify your life.

Long-term and short-term goals

Once you have established your long-term goals, you will have the focus to set short-term goals and to make the everyday choices that follow. If you have that long-term goal of being a patient, loving stepmom, for example, you might set short-term goals that on your stepkids' next visit you will hold your temper and take every opportunity to connect with them in a positive way. Then, when your stepdaughter makes a mess of the bathroom floor, you can respond with your goals in mind. You can either a) get upset or b) make a game of seeing how fast she can clean it up. Which alternative will help you reach your goals?

You get the idea. Be conscious of the opportunities that arise which will help you move toward your goals, and approach them with creativity and humor. Do that all weekend, and you'll have accomplished your short-term goal. Do it until it becomes a habit, and you've met your long-term goal, too. Then your weekends, and your life, will be simpler and more enjoyable. So look far, far ahead, toward a future that you can choose.

Keep your initial goals broad, conceptual, and most of all, meaningful. Select the few things that are truly the most important to you—the things you feel deep, deep down in your heart. Those are the only goals that you will honestly care about reaching. If building a relationship with your in-laws isn't very important to you right now, don't make it a goal just because you think you should. But if getting past the anger you feel toward your stepkids' mom *is* important, write it down, even though you know it will be hard.

Discover what your goals are by paying attention to what occupies your mind night and day. What excites you? What thoughts or activities give you a sense of purpose? What would be the greatest thing you could see yourself doing in five or ten years? Think also about what fills you with dread, makes your stomach knot up, or stands in the way of your happiness. Those feelings, both good and bad, will tell you where you need to do your work. When you can identify what you want to do or change in your life and focus on it clearly, you can move forward to build the life you want.

There's no room or time for noncommittal, wishy-washy, kinda, maybe stuff you might sorta want. Concentrating on just a few goals that are sacred to you makes it easier to stay committed to them. Your goals have to be completely real, even worth fighting for, because sometimes you'll have to do just that. Write the top five long-term goals that relate to your stepfamily here.

My long-term goals:

1. _____
2. _____
3. _____
4. _____
5. _____

As you write down your goals, remember that the first thing you need to figure out is the simple yet profound answer to this question: *what do you want?* Your goals can be broad, but they must not be vague or hard to understand, or you won't be able to reach them. You must know *exactly* what they mean. Only then you will be able to make the choices that will help you reach your goals. Clear, defined goals give you focus, which will lead you to a simpler life.

Does this choice get you closer to your goal?

Once you have established goals for your life, you can start doing the things that will get you closer to them. Instantly. Today! When you have a choice to make, just ask yourself: *does this choice get me closer to my goal?* A "yes" answer means proceed, a "no" means hold on a minute.

Answering that question allows you to take a step forward every time you have the chance. If you're thinking of doing something that won't get you closer to your goal, it's either wrong or a waste of your precious time and energy. But if it will move you in the right direction, have the clarity to recognize that and then the courage to act. Few things will make you happier than proceeding toward your goal. Stepmoms' lives are filled with so many setbacks and even train wrecks that we need every bit of encouragement and forward progress that we can get!

Some opportunities present themselves as short-term goals that you can plan on reaching. Other times, they arrive unexpectedly. I'll give an example of each kind.

One of my long-term goals is to create more "entire family" memories. My husband and the boys often engage in activities that fall way below my interest level (such as going to video arcades, the biggest waste of circuitry I've ever seen). As the lone female at my house, combined with lives so hectic that we don't have much time to do "big" things together, my chances to build "entire family" memories are somewhat limited. I've found that I need to take advantage of opportunities whenever they arise.

One Saturday afternoon, my husband was loading up the kids to grab a burger and then bike some trails in the national forest. My first inclination was to simplify that day by staying home alone! I had plenty of work to keep me busy and I knew I could enjoy the peace and quiet while they were gone. But sometimes the choice that appears more complicated is actually the choice that simplifies your life.

Though I really felt like staying home alone that day, I asked myself the all-important question: *does this choice get me closer to my goal?* In this case, going with them was the better choice.

It also was the choice that meant that they all had to wait while I found my other tennis shoe and rounded up a hat to cover my messy hair, while my husband pumped up my terminally flat bicycle tires. And it meant forcing the boys to fold up like a roadmap so that I'd have a place to sit in the truck. At the time, it seemed the more complicated option. But it wasn't. It was based on a clarity and focus that came from staying true to my goals.

Remaining focused on your goal will help you make these kinds of decisions more easily whenever they present themselves. And focusing on your long-term goals will also help you set your short-term goals.

On another rare day that my family had to spend together, we went to a nearby river canyon with beautiful rock faces to climb, which is one of my favorite things to do. There is one huge rock that's shaped like a mushroom, and climbing is especially difficult when you have to lean backward to do it! My husband and the boys all managed the treacherous climb. I tried and failed a couple of times and had the scrapes to prove it. They encouraged me to keep trying, but I knew I wouldn't make it that day. Without enough upper-body strength (or rappelling gear), I was left by myself, looking from below at the four of them standing triumphantly on top.

I was discouraged, though just being there was a good experience that would help me reach my "entire family memories" goal. But something my younger stepson said led me to establish another short-term goal on the spot, one that will get me even closer to my long-term goal. "Come on, climb up!" he called from the top of the rock. "Then we'll have the whole family up here." Though not being able to make the climb broke my heart, his words washed joy all over me. He wanted *me* up there, too. In his mind, the five of us *are* a "whole family."

I want to climb that rock with them so that I can add a memory of all of us up there together to my collection. Having that as a short-term goal means that I'll have to build my strength so that I'll be able to make the climb when we return to the park. With our schedule, that may take a while, but that's okay. I have a goal, and I know what I need to do to achieve it. (The weight training has already started!)

Without clarity and focus, I might not have understood all of that, nor might I have recognized that there was a lot I could do to gain something very important to me. Now it's pretty simple.

The flip side

In the quest to reach your goals, it's often easiest to see the things that you *shouldn't* do. Criticizing your stepchildren's mother in front of them, for example, will not lead to a pleasant relationship. The kids undoubtedly will tell her everything you said, most likely several times, until she's ready to take out a restraining order against you. In this case, asking *does this choice get me closer to my goal?* has a quick and easy answer, because making negative comments is entirely counterproductive to any goal you may have. Not all of your decisions will be that simple.

For instance, it can be hard to hold your tongue about rude, disrespectful stepchildren, even if you know that complaining to your husband will lead to an argument. It's a real dilemma: You don't want to upset him, but you can't live with the kids behaving the way they are. The answer lies in your goals. If one of your goals is "having a more peaceful home," that probably includes stepchildren who are better-behaved than yours may be. That means dealing with their dad and his reluctance to accept that their behavior needs to change. This is a time when it will be hard *not* to do what you shouldn't do.

If your husband will view your comments as an attack on his kids, the two of you will become divided, and that certainly won't get you closer to your goal. That's why you'll need a different route. Perhaps you could keep a record of the bad or disrespectful behavior and present it to him at a calm time. Or, instead of reacting directly to the kids, say nothing to them and ask your husband what he thinks you should have said and how he would feel in a similar situation. You'll still be working toward your goal, but you'll do it in a simpler, less volatile way. Learning *not* to do the wrong thing is also an important part of reaching your goals.

Choosing your priorities

When you establish your goals, you're also setting priorities, whether you realize it or not. Managing your family is like running a corporation. The financial bottom line is the priority for any business. The long-term health of your family is *your* top priority. You have to make choices based on that first priority, and the smaller ones within it.

You face many decisions every day that may feel like just more burdens on your busy life. In reality, they are the infinite, sustaining, progressive choices that can simplify your days. They are tiny opportunities that propel you either toward or away from your goals. They are part of your power, because you set your own priorities.

As you establish your priorities, answer the question honestly—*does this get me closer to my goal?*—and you'll know what to do. When you understand your priorities, you can protect them.

When your husband hurts you, is it more important to punish him—or to grant forgiveness so that you can move on? Is it more important to nurse your anger, holding it all in—or to approach him and ask for understanding? Which will get you closer to your goal of building a strong marriage? Although marching toward your goals requires constant work and effort, it also brings you closer to the happiness you seek.

When you find yourself struggling among the priorities in your life, remember that your relationships with your husband, children, and stepchildren take precedence over your relationships with your ex-husband and your husband's ex-wife. Sometimes you can get confused. Make the choices that will protect your top priorities.

It may not be easy. For example, you may find yourself having to decide between supporting your husband and pacifying your ex-husband over some matter. A situation that should be simple may appear difficult, leading you to agonize over it far more than you need to. Instead, go back to that all-important question, and regain your focus.

That focus will help you know what to do. Since the process of deciding what to do is often more complicated than the consequences that come later, having a laser-like focus on your goals is vital. When you have clarity about a situation, you can easily choose the solution that will lead toward your goals, saving your energy to deal with the fallout. You will be able to accept whatever comes next and let the rest go, finding strength in knowing that you made the right decision, because it was based on your goals.

You will be amazed at the clarity and focus that come when you ask that one simple question: *does this get me closer to my goal?* You'll come to rely on that seemingly benign question as a framework in which even tiny decisions can be made. Pondering it as you make the less-than-critical decisions that arise every day quickly becomes a habit. The big decisions then become simpler, too.

Even when the choice is between two desirable options, as in my earlier example of riding bikes with the boys or staying home alone, you simplify the debate when you know where your priorities lie. That is profound and powerful. You are in control of what you choose, and you know the reasons behind your choice. You don't have to worry about the process. You can just make a decision and move on.

When priorities conflict

Because we have so many people in our lives and so much to do, sometimes one priority suffers while we progress toward a goal on another. That doesn't mean you won't eventually achieve both. It just means that you're busy, not that you're not truly committed.

So what do you do when you're faced with two good alternatives, each one representing a different priority? You can't attend two children's events at the same time in different places. You can't stay up late for some one-on-one time with your daughter and also snuggle in for an early night with your husband. You have to make a choice, but it doesn't have to be difficult.

First, relax. You can't be in two places at one time. Start simplifying the process by accepting that bit of fact and then move on. I've seen many people wring their hands over the fact that they couldn't do two things at once. How in the world does that simplify anything? It doesn't, but it sure does take up a lot of energy, and we stepmoms don't have any of that to spare.

Next, just make a choice. Sure, you say, but how? It usually will come down to this: what is the better choice *right now*? These kinds of decisions crop up all the time, and we often complicate them more than we need to. Since you'll probably find yourself facing dilemmas like these fairly often, here are a few ways to help you choose what to do:

1. Instinct. What is your "gut feel" about the situation? The sensation that's leaning you one way or the other isn't an inner ear problem. It's that intangible "something" that can feel what you can't see. It's amazing how right your intuition is, if you'll only listen to it. Learn to trust your instinct. Then use it.

2. Logic. It may seem elementary, but ask yourself what is the simplest, most obvious answer to your dilemma. What if someone else were facing this problem—would the answer be easy then? Sometimes we can't see the clear answer because of complications, either real or imagined. Think of the line of reasoning you would use with another person. It will simplify your struggle.

3. Perspective. Realize that although these kinds of conflicts may arise almost every day, they're not monumental. They're just unfortunate. Don't turn them into major life events. Cut through the what-ifs and focus on what happens *after* you've made the choice. This dilemma will come and go, and another will follow. Look into the future, to all of your goals, and see where this situation fits in. Your priorities may conflict once in a while, but choosing one over the other today won't keep you from your goals.

When difficult choices present themselves to you, don't complicate the situation any more than you need to. Instead, listen quietly to your heart. Think it over, make a decision, and then proceed. You'll still be moving toward your goals, even if one of them takes a back seat for a while. That's okay. It's part of life. Simplifying is about keeping those few major goals in mind. Do your best with those, and let everything else go.

Second (and third) chances

Sometimes, despite our best efforts, we make mistakes. We make the wrong choice and we feel as though we've fallen into a deep pit with no way out, then beat up on ourselves while we're down there. Stop it. It's time-consuming and destructive.

Even when you have simplified your life by maintaining focus on a few chosen goals, you'll still have that little inconvenience of every day living to contend with. Besides that, you're human, prone to frustration and fatigue, temper and tantrums. Perhaps building a close relationship with your stepson is one of your very important goals. Though from time to time you'll make a less-than-perfect choice (such as arguing with him over something insignificant because it's one of your pet peeves), you'll have plenty of other opportunities to get closer to him.

Life is long. We foul things up today and, lo and behold, the sun will come up tomorrow and give us a brand new chance to try again. You will have many, *many* opportunities to make good choices that will lead you to your goals. How much fairer can it get?

Stepmothering isn't a sprint, it's a marathon. There will be second, third, tenth, and thirtieth chances to make choices that will lead you toward your goals. The key is to learn from each step that takes you away from a goal, so that you are less likely to repeat it.

Your goals are more of a journey than a destination. Continue to work toward them every chance you get. Things will get simpler when you realize that this is a long process, one filled with changing scenarios and elusive opportunities. When you take the time to ask yourself the question—*does this get me closer to my goal?*—you make your choices simpler.

But when you don't pay enough attention to that question, and the stresses in your life get in the way of your answer, you'll inevitably choose complexity, and painful consequences will follow. Suppose that one of your goals is to better understand how to parent your stepdaughter. If one day you jump to conclusions and believe she's guilty of something that she actually didn't do, you'll feel pretty miserable. Not only that, she'll be hurt and upset, and you'll have to deal with the reverberations that your incorrect assumption created. All is not lost, however.

Although that mistake may not take you directly toward your goal, it is nonetheless valuable. That's because you can learn amazing things from it, even though it hurts. Use your "backsliding" as a teacher to help you clarify your next choice and simplify what follows. Eliminate worry and guilt over any hiccups and move on. More chances are guaranteed. There is much to do; your goal is still there!

Think of some second chances that you've received, and be grateful for them. When your stepdaughter forgives you for jumping to conclusions about her, that's a second chance. Use it. You only fail if you let go of your goal.

Now think of some other poor choices you've made. Can you uncover any second chances hidden there? Don't let them get away. Make use of them to simplify your life.

Relishing clarity, maintaining focus

Your life may be so overwhelming and mind-boggling at times that you'll be tempted to banish any thoughts of the future. Your immediate concerns center around conflicting schedules, dealing with your stepchildren's mother, battles over the differing rules at Mom's house and Dad's house, keeping track of the kids' belongings scattered between their homes, and countless other hassles. All you want to do is get through today, which feels weighed down by heavy obligations that are draining your energy.

You may feel that, far from progressing toward your goals, you're downright marching in the opposite direction. You may just want to say, "Forget it! It's too hard. I can't get *there* when I can't even deal with *here*." Yes, you can. The daily concerns are just part of the package that came with your life. They can be managed. You don't simplify the daily grind by abandoning plans for the future, but by maintaining your focus on the future with simple choices made today. That might sound backward, but it's not. Find the clarity to help you get past today's distractions so that you can accomplish great things with your life.

A clear focus is critical to your survival. You will find simplicity and peace when you stay focused on your goals and keep making the choices that will propel you toward them. Your goals, if chosen wisely, represent the very essence of who you are. You alone choose your goals, and you alone decide how important they are. They are a place where you have total control. Be true to yourself by working toward them. All you have to do is keep going, one step at a time.

I knew I was a stepmom when . . .

. . . the kids started asking me to sign their school papers and fill out their permission slips. I know it seems like a trivial thing, but it occurred to me that they thought of me as a parent when they asked me to do those things for them.

— *Brenda, Ohio, stepmom of three*

. . . my stepson told my soon-to-be mother-in-law that I was "his Annie" and not hers! He was quite possessive of me. I knew he loved me!

—*Ann, stepmom of one son*

. . . I was the one taking time off to go to appointments, bought his clothes, and visited him every other week, five hours from home, while he was in rehab and his mother couldn't be bothered. When I sat on the couch holding him while he cried after his mother told him she never wanted to see him again.

— *Mother of one, stepmom of one*

. . . we were dropping my stepson off at his mother's house and he yelled for "Mom" while we were talking to her. She and I both instinctively answered "What?" I apologized to her and she turned to talk to him. He told his mom that he wasn't talking to her, he was talking to me! I got one of the nastiest looks I have ever seen and told my husband I thought it was time we leave. I realized that day that although my stepson may often think of me as his mother, I will never be his mother.

— *Kim Peterson, mom of two and stepmom of one*

. . . the school told the kids they had to use an experience with their "real" mother for an essay for Mothers Day and my stepchild won an award for it. Since their mom lives out of state and couldn't come to the awards ceremony, I went to the awards committee to ask if they could send her the flowers her child had won. I was taking a backseat and trying to show grace and respect for all.

— *Isabella, New York*

. . . I started sounding like my mother!!!

— *A stepmom from Texas*

. . . the girls' mother put me in my place. The first time she heard her daughter call me "Mama," she called my husband and screamed about how dare we allow her to do this and promote blatant disrespect of her as their biological mother. Again, on Mothers Day, she claimed a "right" to have the girls that whole weekend, as they are the reason she celebrates that day. I know that until these girls come into their own, I will be stepmom, and nothing else. When they are older, they will see that being "Mom" is not a right but a feeling.

— Tracey, stepmom of two

. . . my fiancé's 4 year-old son yelled for me to come upstairs to the bathroom. Upon my arrival, he asked me to please help him wipe.

— Janet B., Pennsylvania

CHAPTER 4

Simplify Your Relationships

Life is a dance, but you can't always lead.

When you were a little girl and someone asked what you wanted to be when you grew up, did you say "a stepmom" or "an ex-wife" or "a second wife"? Get those hands higher; I can't see them! Nobody?

I didn't think so. Yet here you are, not only surrounded by these unnatural relationships you never expected to have, but probably defining yourself by them. But even though becoming a stepmom wasn't part of your original plans, it is the life that you have chosen. With a strong spirit and clear goals, you can simplify the complicated relationships that came along with it.

Relationships in a stepfamily are never easy. You make repairs to your heart and requests for sanity on a daily basis. Your future is clouded by the past, and your present seems to exist at the whim of others. You may think, for example, that talking your way out of an IRS audit would be easier than coming to an agreement with your stepchildren's mom. True, you may not be able to make her sing your praises far and wide. But you *can* simplify your relationship with her.

You can do the same with all the other people in your life—yes, the same ones who continually misunderstand, misrepresent, misuse, and misguide you. Take heart. Although you can't change someone else, you can change *yourself,* replacing fear and resentment with security and growth. You can manage the challenging parts of your relationships and enjoy the fulfilling parts.

What kinds of changes do you want to make in your family relationships? Whether you want to repair your relationship with your ex-husband or build a relationship with your husband's ex-wife, grow closer to a stepchild or enrich your marriage, you can enhance your efforts by controlling what's yours to control. You can simplify these very complicated relationships with the powers of *perspective, restraint, abundance,* and *forgiveness.* We'll get to these soon. But first, let's take a look backward, just for a moment.

Look back, but just once

One reason that stepfamily relationships can be so difficult is that they often are tied to a complex and painful past. Becoming a stepmom certainly wasn't a route you expected your life to take. Your personal history, though, and the relationships that came from it, remain a part of who you are, and your husband's past and his relationships will always be with him. That's a lot of baggage for one marriage to carry. To survive and grow, you must be able to put the past behind you and focus on the future's potential and promise.

But before you can move forward to have the kind of family you want, you must accept the past. You only complicate your life when you view the past as if it were a play for which you could write a new ending. It's elementary physics: you can't control what already has happened. Instead, you must accept the difficult parts of your lives and reconcile your feelings about events and people so that your focus is on healing, not hurting. Treat the past, and the relationships it created, as cast in stone:

You can't change the fact that your husband was once married to another woman.

You can't change the fact that your husband is loyal to the children they had together.

You can't change the fact that you may have suffered your own divorce or broken relationship.

You can't change the fact that your ex-husband may still be in your life because of children *you* had together.

You can't change these facts, but you can change your *attitude*—from resentment to acceptance, from despair to promise. The goal is to spend your energy moving toward the future, rather than reliving the past. It's a simple yet powerful choice.

Tales from the Blender

Realize that your presence is painful to the ex-wife beyond anything you can imagine. You have taken her place. That hurts. Her children will talk about you when they go home to her. That hurts. Her children may be affectionate with you in front of her. That hurts. Her children may prefer to sit on your lap instead of hers at a function you both attend. That *really* hurts. As annoying and bitchy as she may be, remember that almost everything that you do with her kids is a threat to her and hurts her. Some moms are more mature than others, but all are hurt by the presence of the stepmom at some point. You must be compassionate.

— *Kathi O., stepmom and mom-to-be*

Sometimes we hold on to grudges and anger and hurts far too long. We grasp on to everything that's ever happened to us as if our lives depend on it. But in this case, our lives depend on letting go. You'll never fulfill the best of your future if you continue to be haunted by the past. You can let it go if you choose to, even if that seems impossible.

You don't have to approve of everything that happened in the past or justify it or like it. Just accept it. Mending family relationships and building new ones all at once is difficult. You make it even tougher when you fight the past instead of reconciling yourself to it. Acknowledge events that have happened and move on. Bear in mind that although the past won't ever go away completely, it does become farther and farther *in the past* every day.

Focus on what lies within your control—and let go of anything that doesn't. It is *not* in your control to change the past, even the ugly parts that you've been grieving over for months or even years. It is *not* in your control to eliminate all awkward encounters. It is *not* in your control to change other people, much as you might like to do that in some cases! Instead, you can adjust your attitude to help yourself. *That* is well within your control.

Tales from the Blender

My husband has had total responsibility for his son since he was an infant. He is fiercely proud of that, and takes any inference that things could be done differently as a personal insult. We do discuss things, but it's mostly to let me know how things are going to be done. It has become obvious that what he wants is for someone to raise his son *his* way, and to keep her own ideas about parenting to herself. I am in the process of turning all parenting responsibility back to him. It is difficult, because I know I could do better, but I must back off and let father and son sink or swim.

— *A stepmom from Pennsylvania*

Though the past is already written, you control a part of your future when you simplify the everyday interactions with the people in your life. There are four powers that you can use to simplify your relationships, starting right now. Even if they have little visible effect on anyone else, they are mighty nonetheless because of what they give to *you*. These powers enable you to overcome extraordinary challenges and difficult people and concentrate instead on what is most important to you: working toward your goals. Use these powers every day and be amazed at the peace they breathe into your life.

First, the power of perspective

I'm not about to tell you that dealing with your new family won't hurt from time to time. Nor am I going to say that you should be able to ignore criticisms and misunderstandings. What I am going to ask you to do is to keep it all in perspective. Take the pressure off yourself to repair, build, or even understand your relationships right away.

Losing perspective is much too easy for any stepmom. It's almost impossible not to lose sight of your goals when you're laboring in the trenches day to day. There are too many people to please and too many places to fail. Sometimes you *do* fail. At those times, the relationships that define your life may begin to look like prison bars. It becomes hard to find one single reason to keep facing such overwhelming challenges, and even harder to believe that you will ever accomplish any of your goals. That's when you have to get some perspective and regain control over this part of your life.

One failure will not destroy your relationship. You are living proof that people get second chances and that something very good can come out of very sad circumstances. Not everything is a tragedy, so don't get stuck in your missteps. I used to let one misspoken word ruin an entire weekend, until I saw that this was not only a terrible waste of time and energy, it showed a lack of faith in myself and my family. Later, when I reviewed what had happened more objectively, I could see that in the big picture of our lives together, this was a tiny dot. I realized that we could overcome this and any future mini-crises.

Don't let little problems consume you. Stop, take a breath, look at each episode for what it is, and don't turn it into anything more. If you really do act like a wicked stepmother on a given day, that isolated event need not cloud the vision you have for your family. Put the issue into its proper perspective, and then get back to your life. Keep focused on repairing and building your relationships and on reaching your goals. Don't get sidetracked by the misunderstandings and hurt feelings that happen in every life.

Your mistakes may *feel* bigger because you're a stepmom, but they're not. They're actually lessons on the way to your goals. When you view your mistakes as learning tools, they become far less threatening. Use them to move closer to your goals, instead of farther away. Your power of perspective will get you through the tough times. Stay focused on the learning, not the failing.

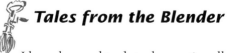

Tales from the Blender

I have learned to detach emotionally from my stepkids. That doesn't mean I don't love them and care about them; it means I am not emotionally invested in them the same way I am with my biological children. When my stepkids mess up, as children inevitably do, I don't have to take it personally or feel like it's all my fault. They have two parents, and I'm not one of them. That realization alone was a great relief.

— *Polly Bywater, Tulsa, Oklahoma, mom of four, stepmom of five, custodial of two*

Second, the power of restraint

We want to excel in this role so much that sometimes we just don't know when to stop, even when what we're witnessing has nothing to do with us. That's another way we complicate our lives. Perhaps there's a situation between your husband and his ex-wife that has nothing to do with you. Yes, I know that everything they do affects you in some way, but like it or not, some of their interactions do not require your blessing. By getting overly involved, you may only create problems, both for yourself and for them, where none existed before. You simplify your life greatly by working only on the problems that are yours alone to solve.

When you are tempted to become enmeshed in a situation that doesn't directly concern you, ask yourself, *Is what I'm about to add helpful and nonjudgmental?* If the answer to either part of this question is *no,* then use your power of restraint and stay out of it. The first part is pretty obvious: only get involved if you have something useful to contribute. But you may wonder about the second. Why do you need to be nonjudgmental as well? The answer is that when you judge someone else's life, you complicate your own. This will take a little time to explain, but hang in there.

As you know, much of our stress as stepmoms comes from being uncertain whether we can succeed in this role. Since we're insecure, we get defensive. We lash out at what we see as the reason things are so difficult for us. In many cases, that's our stepchildren's mom. We project our fears and insecurities on her, and we're quick to judge everything she does. We've complicated things, and now we worry even more: we fear that she is judging us.

Let's say, for example, that you want to build a closer relationship with your stepson. As you try to figure out how to do that, you'll probably watch his interactions with his own mother and start comparing your parenting abilities to hers.

Since you lack confidence in yourself, you're likely to assume that she is evaluating you at the same time.

That may be the case, and it may not. Being judged by the people in your life, especially your husband's ex-wife, certainly is uncomfortable. But whether or not someone else is judging you should make no difference, because you alone remain responsible for your actions. The same can be said when you are tempted to make judgments about another person. Judging leads to involvement, and you don't need the extra worry. By refraining from judging someone else, you draw the line between what is yours and what is not.

Asking yourself whether your involvement is *nonjudgmental* will tell you whether you are truly being helpful or are simply trying to change someone whose actions you disapprove of. Perhaps you don't care for the clothes that your stepkids' mom buys for them. Maybe they don't fit well or seem inappropriate for their ages. Will it do any good to complain about her selections, and will she even listen to your opinions? If not, this is a place to let go and not spend any time and energy on the issue. Focus on the decisions that you *need* to make instead of involving yourself where you don't have to. Less involvement equals fewer complications.

Your priority is to tend to your own responsibilities, not to judge others. When you exercise your power of restraint and stop making judgments, you make your relationships much simpler. You can accept what others do without feeling a need to approve of it. You also grant yourself the same permission— to make decisions without someone else's stamp of approval.

Fight your own battles, and let your husband and everyone else fight theirs. When you draw a very bold line between what you need to pass judgment on and what you don't, you simplify everything. Return your focus to *your* goals, and don't be distracted by your opinions about others or theirs of you. You've chosen your path. That's where you need to spend your energy, time, and talents.

It may be especially hard to withhold judgment in one unfortunate situation. That's when your stepkids' mom tells lies about you. In that situation, passing judgment still won't solve the problem. You won't improve your relationships with either the mom or the kids by speaking ill of her. Instead, use your power of restraint and find a more constructive approach.

If you can prove that she's not telling the truth, let the evidence speak for you. If it's a "she said, she said" situation, defend yourself without attacking her. I know that's hard, but as you simplify your life as a stepmom, you'll quickly discover that the best path is one that helps you find peace inside yourself. That often means practicing a restraint you didn't even know you were capable of. Give it a try. If you can be satisfied with your side of the equation during a confrontation or in the face of an injustice, that's all that matters.

Tales from the Blender

What surprised me the most about becoming a stepmom was the games that kids play to pit you against their mother. It's almost like they want you to hate each other. I finally began to turn it around by really watching what I said. Instead of getting mad over what my stepdaughter said or did, I would sympathize with her mother. I also would say things that would look like I agreed with her mother. Apparently, my kind words made it back to her mom, and *her* tune changed, too. She started to call and speak to me about the child, instead of just asking for my husband in a huffy, irritated-that-I-answered-the-phone voice.

— *Jodi Staten, Arkansas*

So how do you acquire this power of restraint when you're hurting and want to lash out? First of all, realize that it is within your control. You can use this power all by yourself, every day. Practice restraint in little ways at first and then, as you begin to see the benefits, extend it to bigger issues. Then watch your relationships improve. Go ahead and offer advice if you're asked, clear up a misunderstood fact if you can, but otherwise, try very hard to stay out of things that don't concern you directly. Instead, put your energy into the things that do. There are plenty of those around, and focusing on them is what will get you closer to your goals.

Tales from the Blender

I have disengaged from having any type of relationship with my stepchildren's mother. No matter how courteously I behaved, she viewed me as a threat to her own motherhood and ability to parent. Realizing I could never gain her respect and friendship has given me a new outlook on stepparenting. I simply do the best I can do with the children when they are here, and I don't worry about the rest.

— *Denise, custodial stepmom of two*

I have by no means yet found growth and peace. I have merely developed the ability to hold my tongue when jealousy gets the better of me and accept that I chose to follow this path.

— *Lucinda Green, United Kingdom*

Third, the power of abundance

Many stepfamily relationships are strained because resources are stretched—time, money, you name it. Although a large portion of your resource allocation is probably out of your control, you may have a hard time letting go. The issues are just too volatile and they hit you where it really hurts. You can simplify them, though, when you approach shortages in a new way, with the power of abundance.

You no doubt have heard this bit of wisdom: it's not what happens to us that determines our happiness, but our *attitude* about what happens to us. That is especially sound advice when it comes to your family's resources. By following it, you remove one huge threat to almost all relationships: jealousy.

Jealousy makes you focus on exactly what you should not—what you don't have, instead of what you do. When you are jealous, you feel anything but in control. Jealousy makes you petty and unproductive. It takes your focus away from your goals and sits on you heavily, like a mound of wet wool. You can't grow yourself and your family when you're paralyzed with envy, bitter and resentful of what others have that you don't. Understand why these feelings invade your heart so easily and vow to get rid of them, with the power of abundance.

Money. Issues related to money can make a mess of your relationships more quickly than almost anything else. Even in stepfamilies with plenty of it to go around, money is often a source of conflict because it equals power in many people's eyes.

Some financial issues may have been decided well before you entered the picture. Alimony or child support, for example, are facts that you most likely just have to accept. It's easy for stepmoms to resent the money given to their stepchildren's mom, especially if they lack things they need for their own homes. Those feelings can tear you up unless you come to terms with the situation. If the payments are truly unfair, I encourage you and your husband to seek a legal remedy. If not, accept them and move on by changing your focus from one of lack to one of abundance.

Find value in relationships, not money. It's a simple idea, but it's powerful. Since leading a simpler life means finding and focusing on what is most important to you, concentrate your energy on what you have gained, not what you have lost. You have the marriage you wanted. It came with challenges, but you can meet them.

I encourage you to tackle issues up front as much as possible. A definite plan for allocating money before situations arise is, of course, the easiest way to avoid problems. Set a budget, even if you have plenty of money, so that you know where it is going. When new issues come up, such as college costs or cars for your teens, make joint decisions about them. Don't be afraid to address financial issues while they are still small. The only way to simplify your money concerns is to reveal all of them.

I don't want to sound like Pollyanna, but you actually can use cash shortages as opportunities to bring your family closer together. Anything you have in common with those who share your home, even a need for creative financing, can be used to your advantage. A simple, honest, "Money's tight this weekend, so let's see who can come up with the best entertainment that's absolutely free!" says that the family is a unit, that together you can solve problems, and that all of you can depend on each other. It's also an excellent way to show the kids what you truly value.

Tales from the Blender

In the beginning, we received permission for the children to live with us, but we still were supposed to provide child support checks to the "ex." It was really hard during those times. We couldn't get food stamps, medical cards, or welfare because we were not the "custodial" parents. We lived from paycheck to paycheck those first three years. The kids always ate first. When they outgrew their shoes, I gave them mine so they would always have something on their feet. I let my stepdaughter wear my tops when she wanted to. In spring, I would cut down all but one pair of their jeans into shorts and put a hem on them to make them look store-bought. The kids were always clean, fed, and taken care of no matter what the situation brought. I never thought that seven years later they would remember the years when we struggled, but they do.

— *Isabella, New York*

I have a budget for every month, and I know exactly how much I can spend. I had to learn to get organized!

— *A stepmom from Texas*

Finances will be a problem in any marriage, but in a second marriage, they are amplified by the constant outflow of child support, visitation expenses, birthdays, holidays, etc. I believe wholeheartedly that husband and wife should keep their finances separate. It's vital that the couple discuss their finances in detail, with very clear expectations as to who pays what to whom.

— *Polly Bywater, Tulsa, Oklahoma, mom of four, stepmom of five, custodial of two*

Time. Time is another resource that is stretched in a stepfamily. You'll have time issues that traditional families never think about. Your time to be a family will be infringed upon, and at times overshadowed, by the children's other families. Time for you and your husband to be alone may be impacted by his kids or your kids or a crisis elsewhere in the family. Time that your husband spends with his children may seem like a party to which you're not invited. Too many sets of grandparents means too many decisions to make about holidays and other extended family gatherings. All of these time pressures strain your relationships even more and make building and protecting them that much harder.

Time is a valuable resource, so simplifying your relationships will help you to make better use of the time you have. Here's how.

First, look at the long term. In many ways, your life is just beginning. Focus on the abundance of opportunities you have now, the "forevermore" that you've given yourself with this marriage. Amid all of the daily intrusions on your time, there still are many opportunities to grow your family. Nowhere does making each moment count matter more than in a stepfamily.

Next, focus on the time you have instead of the time you don't. You don't have the luxury of time to spend on hurt feelings, anger, guilt, or anything else that isn't a productive use of your hours and days. Use the time you have, even when it's interrupted or insufficient, to take a tiny step forward. If you can appreciate the time you are together, no matter how insufficient it is, you won't worry about the amount of time you're apart.

You may have to become very creative about your schedule, since it is often dictated by the whims of others. If one plan won't work because of someone else's decision, have another one ready. Flexibility is key. At unexpected moments, you may find yourself with an opportunity to spend time with your stepdaughter when you had planned to do errands, or to have an evening alone with your husband when you thought you'd be shuttling the kids a dozen different places. Don't waste any chance to get closer to your family, even when time is very limited. Even tiny bits of conversation that take only a minute can strengthen the bonds you're working to build.

The resource of time can complicate any relationship. None of us has enough of it to devote to everything that we need and want. Though abundance of time is not possible, an abundance of *opportunity* is a reality—*your* reality. Remember that, even when you feel that opportunities to grow your family are nearly nonexistent. Seize every chance that presents itself. Your relationships will grow and improve when you make wise use of your time. Focus on what you can control, in whatever time you have. It's quite a bit.

Tales from the Blender

I went into the stepmother role with the delusion that I could go from being a single woman with no kids to a stepmother of three without sacrificing my work or my sanity. It only took a few months to realize that something had to change. My husband and I decided that although we needed my income, our family life was more important and that we would have to compromise. I was lucky to have the opportunity to change my working hours to accommodate the kids' schedules. I now work from 8:30 a.m. to 2:30 p.m. so that I can be home when the youngest gets off the bus. It has relieved my stress considerably. It also has given me time alone with them to get to know them and truly be a part of their lives.

— *Brenda, Ohio, stepmom of three*

We have our oldest help out when we have to run errands. As far as housework goes, we all make the mess, we all clean the mess! That saves me *lots* of time!

— Angie, mom of two and stepmom of two

When we have my stepson, our time together as a family is sacred. We all have to check with each other before we schedule something that takes away time from the family. It would be nice if we didn't have to pay child support, but it's just one of those things that I don't have control over. Rather than my husband working more or working overtime, which could result in even higher child support, I have taken an on-call job, in addition to my regular job, that has supplemented our family income quite well. I only take call shifts on days that he's working, so it never takes away time from us!

— Ann, stepmom of one son

Focus on what your family *does* have—the opportunities and choices—instead of dwelling on limitations and jealousy. Let the kids in on the situation in a way that says, "We've got some problems, but we're going to solve them ourselves." They, too, will begin to see that there is always something more, always an abundance, if you only take the time to search for it. It is a simple step that you can take to minimize some of the difficulties that stem from stretched resources. The results will be worth the effort.

When you approach these issues as a team, the search for solutions unites your family with confidence and loyalty. Let any scarcity of resources inspire you to strengthen your relationships by learning to turn to each other. Even money challenges can help you find abundance in your life. Use the abundant resources you do have. Keep your focus there and your family will thrive.

Fourth, the power of forgiveness

Forgiveness has magical powers. It can help you heal the most broken of relationships and give you much-needed peace. We sometimes are reluctant to give or receive forgiveness, afraid that it's not fair or that we're not deserving. But that's not what matters. Forgiveness is about growth and possibility, about trusting in a brighter future in spite of an ugly past. It's about healing for ourselves and simplicity for our relationships. It's possibly the greatest power you have.

Since becoming a stepmom, I've realized that forgiveness is a very important part of who I am. But that doesn't mean it comes easy. I don't know which is harder—forgiving someone else or forgiving myself. It does seem to get easier the older I get, or maybe I'm just becoming more tolerant. What is in front of me now seems far more important that what is behind me. I'm more willing to let go of the past and choose the positive road.

Forgiveness can be difficult for a stepmom, because she's trying so hard to protect what she has achieved. Forgiveness for a former spouse, for example, may seem like weakness or lack of commitment. In reality, it shows true strength. Forgiving herself when she fails may seem like apathy or greed. In reality, it's life-giving, enabling her to save her energy for tomorrow. Forgiveness doesn't endanger what you've worked so hard to get. Instead, it helps ensure its survival.

"But I'm *hurting*," you say. Of course it hurts when someone betrays you or ignores you or abandons you. Though you try to avoid it, the volatile relationships that have been formed because of your marriage guarantee that someone will get hurt from time to time. Often that someone will be you, because you're caught in the absolute middle of it all. I know that you can't just will the pain away. It hurts too much. But you can use your power of forgiveness and the blessings of time to help heal your wounds.

Forgiveness for others. One of the most powerful steps in building your new family relationships is to forgive others when they hurt you. This simplifies your relationships, as well as your life, because hurting takes up a great deal of your energy. Once you've forgiven the hurt, you can start to heal, and then you can direct your energy into more productive paths. When you use your power of forgiveness, you give yourself permission to move forward.

What if you don't believe that the other person deserves your forgiveness? You don't need to make that judgment; whether or not they deserve to be forgiven is beside the point. When you choose to forgive someone who has hurt you, you simplify that relationship *for yourself*, regardless of any benefit the other person receives. You are the one who will benefit most by granting forgiveness.

To receive forgiveness from someone you have forgiven is one of life's greatest blessings. But don't let that be your motivating factor. You may feel that you are not forgiven as often as you forgive, and without a doubt, some people are harder to forgive than others. You may have to work very hard, for example, to forgive your stepchildren's mom for some of the things she does. And even when you do, your hurt feelings won't instantly disappear. But that's not the point. Forgiving her simply means that you're willing to let go, to put unpleasant things in the past. That's what is best for *you*, regardless of her reaction.

With your husband, on the other hand, you may want to forgive right away, but you may not know how, when your relationship is strained and feelings are raw. Look past the act of forgiving to how you will feel afterward. Focus on what came *before* and what will come *after* this incident: feelings of love and acceptance and hope. Isolate the hurt so that you can forgive it and begin to heal from it.

Tales from the Blender

I was anxious to become the typical American nuclear family—mom, dad, and kids (my husband has custody). But when the ex-wife decided she wanted to see the children, my fragile fantasy family was shattered into a million pieces. I was forced to listen to how much the kids adored her, even though she had abandoned them for an adulterous relationship. It was a challenge to learn to smile, pretend it didn't bother me, and control my tongue when I wanted to criticize her.

The love they have for their mother remains, and I no longer try to do anything to come between them. I am not jealous of her any more, as I once was. There is enough love for everyone to share. My life is much happier and more peaceful now that I have learned to manage my relationships with the children and their mother. It is still a struggle, but it is getting easier day by day.

— *Denise, custodial stepmom of two*

Forgiveness for yourself. What about the times when you are the one who has inflicted pain? As hard as you try, your human imperfections do surface from time to time. Someone may be hurting because of something you said or something you did and all you feel is guilt. How do you get beyond that and back on track? Strange as it may sound, your goals are what will help you accept forgiveness for yourself.

Anything that is important enough to be one of your goals is worth your total devotion. Guilt and self-blaming make you lose your focus. They block you from moving forward by keeping you mired in the past. If you want to replace feelings of remorse with feelings of motivation, accomplishment, and satisfaction, don't waste time dwelling on what you should or shouldn't have done. Rectify the situation. Seek forgiveness from the person you've hurt, and then, perhaps hardest of all, forgive yourself. Then quickly return to pursuing your goals.

Maybe you don't think you deserve your own forgiveness. That, too, is irrelevant. You can't work on tomorrow if you're carrying the added weight of yesterday's and today's mistakes. Accept that you will fail, perhaps miserably at times. Then be grateful for the second chances that keep coming. Simplify your relationships—especially your relationship with yourself—with forgiveness, and watch your goals come closer and closer.

Now, *that's* magic.

Tales from the Blender

Say you are sorry when you are wrong! No one is perfect and there is no reason to make yourself look perfect—especially in the eyes of your children. They already love you! If you do something or say something that is wrong, set things straight. If you need to say you are sorry, do it. Even if it means admitting fault to your child!

— *A stepmom from Texas*

A *surprising strength*

Anyone who doubts that God has a sense of humor only has to look at a stepmom.

She finds herself in the most impossible of circumstances, with all the people in her life watching her flounder. Then, as if she isn't unsettled enough, they keep disrupting her life to accommodate theirs, just to be sure she's really paying attention to that comedy of errors in which she stars. No wonder so many of us need a very long vacation!

But that's just fine. We're stronger than we thought, and we become even stronger every day that we continue to build a happy, healthy family. If we can make peace with the people in our lives, our relationships will no longer be the chaotic mess that some may think they are.

Be proud of the commitments you've made. Your husband, your children, and your stepchildren are now your main concern. Take care of those relationships. Then, if you choose to do so, you can address your relationships with your ex-husband, your husband's ex-wife, your new in-laws, and all of the other people in your life. Putting your primary family first will simplify a great deal.

You know, we stepmoms could become downright boring if we just simplified our relationships, minded our own business, and kept making steady progress toward our goals. That might not rate us a spot on the eleven o'clock news, but it sure would bring each of us a more peaceful, enjoyable life. I don't know about you, but I'll take it.

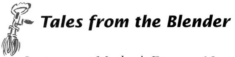 ## *Tales from the Blender*

Last year at Mother's Day, my 13 year-old stepson played in a soccer game. At halftime, the boys came across the field with carnations in their hands for their moms. My wonderful stepson had two carnations. After giving the first to his mother, he brought me a carnation and delivered it with a hug. It was all I could do to fight back the tears!

— *Jennifer Dillman, Kentucky, mom of two*
(so far) & stepmom of two

CHAPTER 5

Simplify Your Communication

Listen carefully, speak softly, act nobly.

We often hear that we live in the Information Age, and that sounds about right. After all, we can communicate throughout the world in a split second. We can uncover and share information as never before. We can connect with anyone, anytime.

Well, almost anyone. You may find it easier to reach a stranger in Kyrgyzstan than to speak in with someone in your own home. There the art of communication is encumbered by the preconceptions and misconceptions that every member has strapped to his or her back like the hump on a camel. You can't seem to eliminate the confusion, and those other people in your family—well, they just won't listen!

Your own intentions are nothing short of noble: to be open and honest and to orchestrate such a sensible, reasonable dialogue among everyone that there are no misunderstood motives or misspoken words. Then why is it that you feel you have to choose your words oh-so-carefully with everyone in your family? And how come it comes out all wrong anyway?

You probably already know that communicating effectively with each other is one of your stepfamily's biggest challenges. Like strangers trapped together on a deserted island, your family will have to figure out what works for you. Given enough time and opportunity, you will learn to trust, communicate, and grow together. You *will* develop the bonds that traditional families have; you'll just have to go through more to get there. But don't give up. It will get easier every day.

Simple, effective communication is not a pointless or unreachable goal but, as with so much else, the route you take toward it must pass through the areas that you can control. There are no magic words that will compel others to agree with you, and you won't ever eliminate all misunderstandings. But you can make things better when you base your communication on your core truths. We'll talk about how to do that in just a bit. But first, let's look at two types of communication—really *mis*communication—that may be all too familiar.

Causes and effects of poor communication

The causes and the effects of strained, ineffective communication are often the same, and it's hard to tell which came first. It's like a garden with a stream of recycled water. Add just a small amount of toxic chemicals and the entire stream becomes contaminated. The gardener needs to interrupt the flow, replace the water, and get the stream flowing again. Poisoned communication, too, feeds on itself and spreads. To repair the damage to your family, you must stop what you're doing, send out a new message, and begin over again. The renewed cycle produces more effective communication.

There are two patterns of poor communication that often appear in stepfamilies. You can prevent both of them from poisoning your home.

Withdrawal. It starts when the only communication between you and your husband is a fight. Your feelings are hurt, or you get so angry that it makes you cry. To protect yourself from even more pain, you withdraw into a shell that allows only room for your own interpretation, right or wrong, of what has been happening. You've entered a damaging cycle.

Because you can't communicate, you withdraw. But because you've withdrawn, you can't communicate. With no understanding coming in and none getting out, there can be no effective communication between the two of you.

The same thing can happen with your stepchildren. They say something you don't understand or that hurts your feelings, and you withdraw to protect yourself. You become overly sensitive to anything they say, your relationship is strained, and you withdraw even more each day. The complications have multiplied.

As damaging as a withdrawal cycle can be, it is not terribly difficult to repair. Since withdrawal arises out of fear and insecurity, the cycle can be broken when you have the strength to be compassionate and consistent with your core truths. (We'll talk about those later in this chapter.) For example, if one of your truths is that you trust the love that you and your husband have, build on that. Obviously, you can't reach a goal of improving your marriage if you don't talk to your spouse. Reach out to him, instead of inward to your pain.

The next time you find yourself withdrawing from your family, vow to end the cycle before it starts. Do these five things:

❖ Approach the problem as if it were a brand new one. Put withdrawal in the past and decide that you will actively seek a solution, right now.

❖ Focus on the positive by relating the problem to one of your goals. For example, one of your goals may be to be a good stepmom. Withdrawing from your stepchildren keeps you from getting closer to your goal.

❖ Reach out. To heal the rift, you have to understand the other person's point of view.

❖ Examine *your* communication in the issue. Has it been unclear? Discover which of your truths you're not communicating and resolve to do so.

❖ Assess your efforts. Pay attention to the process and note what works. The next time you want to pull away from a conflict, think about past successes and incorporate them into your plans.

Mindreading. It's an understandable pitfall for step-moms. Since you're always having to think of everything for everyone in your family, you think that you know what's going on in their minds. You re-write family scenarios based on what you imagine has happened, instead of what actually was said or not said. The problem is that when you respond to what you *assume* others are thinking, the only things you communicate are anger, hurt feelings, and more mistaken assumptions.

There are two kinds of mindreading, and I don't know which one got me into more trouble. I've labeled them "attempted" and "expected." The first are the times I tried to read my family's minds. Too often, all someone had to do was send one word or one glance in my direction and I filed a mental dissertation about what he was thinking and feeling and how he would think and feel for the next forty years. And when that happened, more often than not, I completely missed what actually was going on above the shoulders.

Then there's the companion ailment, when I expected my family to read *my* mind. Even when I thought I was as obvious as a billboard, putting my message so far out there that I thought they might trip over it, my family would fail to get it. I was wrong on both counts, and pain and confusion and more complications abounded as a result.

Mindreading brings you nothing but absolute fatigue. So stop trying to be psychic. Instead, open your ears.

When we resort to mindreading, it's because we have failed to *listen* to our family members. That's unfair to everyone. You want them to listen to your words. Grant them the same courtesy and save everyone a lot of complications. Instead of assuming that you know how someone else feels, ask for clarification. When you listen well, you'll find the understanding you seek.

Faulty communication stems from one of two things: being unsure of how you feel, or being unable to make that clear to others. When you are completely clear about yourself, you have the power and strength you need. Then and only then will you be able to communicate effectively with others. When you fail in these areas, communication fails and your family suffers. Communicate who you are and simplify this part of your life.

Let's find out how to do that.

Your discoveries

I once made a list of my family's biggest communication issues. It was easy: the problems were all my husband's fault! It was a nice little delusion for a while, and that kind of narrow-minded thinking escalated the communication problems we had during the first three years of our marriage.

Finally, in revelation or maybe desperation, I admitted that our problems might possibly, maybe, just a tiny bit, partly be my fault. Sometimes I spent way too much time listening to my own misguided interpretation of events, instead of talking with and listening to my husband. Sometimes I was as clear as a politician in saying what I needed to say. Sometimes I even lied about how I felt, because the truth was too painful to admit. The results were a textbook case of dysfunctional communication, a prelude to divorce court, and way too many nights spent crying myself to sleep.

I loved this man. How could we have gotten into such

huge arguments about things, especially the *same* things, over and over again? The answer turned out to be pretty simple: in this new and complicated way of life, I didn't know who I was any more. My former life was gone and my security in knowing who I was had gone with it.

Once upon a time, when my life was much simpler, I knew how to let others know who I was. But in a new stepfamily, it can be terribly hard to *be* who you really are—much less communicate that to the strangers who now share your home. Before I could do that, I had to re-examine the core truths about myself in light of my new life. Becoming a stepmom forced to me re-learn who I was.

What I thought was a curse actually turned out to be a blessing. Through my re-evaluation, I found renewed strength and a deeper understanding of myself. Only then could I improve my communication with my husband and family. It was a discovery that I would not have had the courage to make if I hadn't realized the frailty and vulnerability of my most important goal—the success of my new marriage and family. Rediscovering myself again was a true gift, one that simplified my days, eased my overloaded mind, and paved the path to my goal.

Your responsibilities

You will improve your communication with your family when you keep in mind two things that are your responsibility:

Show them who you are.
Show them with compassion and consistency.

In other words, first you must be clear about how you feel and what you want, and then you must be compassionate and consistent in the way you express yourself to others. *Compassion* is important because your family members are dealing with many of the same hurts and anxieties that you are. *Consistency* is important because successful communication grows and builds upon itself. These are both your goal and your solution. And everything you need to do these two things is entirely within your control.

With these cornerstones of honesty, compassion, and consistency, you can begin to build the foundation upon which every one of your communications can be based. Everything—your responses, your attitudes, and your reactions—can reflect the truths you've learned about yourself. There's no need to search for new answers every day. Just use what you know to simplify your communication.

When you use this approach, the results will astound you. The interactions between you and your family members will require much less work. Simplicity follows, because our lives are simpler when we have less to worry about.

When you honestly share yourself with your family in a compassionate and consistent way, you build trust. You then will be able to rely on that trust as you tackle your family's problems. Make good choices with your communication so that instead of struggling to understand each other, you can focus on finding solutions together.

Tales from the Blender

We set ground rules early on that everyone had the right to express their feelings, as long as they weren't expressed in anger or to be hurtful. This has done wonders for our relationships! My stepson knows that he has a safe environment to talk about anything that is bothering him. We have made it clear that we will always listen to what each other has to say without being judgmental or critical. This can be difficult at times, but it has led to an incredible relationship among all of us! We have great communication and I know my stepson feels heard.

— Ann, stepmom of one son

Why it matters

I bet you have a pretty tricky question for me right now: "Communication is a two-way street, so how is only working on what *I* can control going to help solve my *family's* communication problems?" Never fear, the answer is right there, in your approach.

Showing who you are means presenting your real self to your family. It means relating to them in a way that reflects the core truths about who you are and what makes you tick.

You may wonder what all of that has to do with your communication as stepmom and second wife. I'll tell you in one word: everything!

If you hide who you are, you're cheating yourself and everyone else. Your family can't know how to relate to you if they don't know who you truly are. By revealing your true self, you'll reduce the confusion, frustration, and resentment that poor communication creates. If you want to simplify your life, your communication must reflect who you are.

For example, if saying a blessing at mealtimes is important to you, but it's not a part of your stepchildren's routine, you may wonder how to deal with that difference in habits. Which of these would better reflect your truths: ignoring your needs while resentment builds inside you, or explaining your needs and reaching a solution? Looking at the situation from that perspective, the answer is clear.

That's not a life-altering example, but you get the idea. If you don't communicate effectively with your family about issues that are important to you, you'll become embittered and annoyed. Besides that, since you've hidden yourself, your family won't even know that you're hurting. Communicating your needs doesn't mean you'll always get your way, of course. You (and the rest of your family) often will need to compromise. The goal is to communicate in a way that can lead to satisfactory solutions to the dilemmas in your home. That requires an honest, compassionate, and consistent approach.

Tales from the Blender

My happiest moment as a stepmom came during a weekend visit. My stepdaughter referred to me as "Mom." She started to correct herself, but then said, "So what? I can call you 'Mom' if I want. This isn't my mom's house, so who cares? Daddy always tells me to do what is in my heart." I agree with this smart little 6 year-old.

— *Tracey, stepmom of two*

Choose your battles wisely, with your spouse, the children, and the ex-wife. Not every issue is worth fighting about. Sometimes you just have to suck it up, let it go, and move on. Life is not always fair. Better learn that quick.

— *Kathi O., stepmom and mom-to-be*

The truths about you

To adequately convey basic truths about yourself to your family members, you first have to know what they are. And you could be in for some surprises. Even if you think you know yourself pretty well, you're going to discover new or expanded truths about yourself *because* of your family. That's okay. The better you know yourself, the better you can communicate with others. Some of my own truths have been better defined to me because of my role as stepmom. I'll give you an example.

In the last chapter, we talked about the power of forgiveness. That's always been important to me, and I believed that I had truly practiced it in my relationships. But when I had to apply it to my new life, it was a whole new ballgame. On a daily basis, I now had to deal with foreign and frightening situations that called for real forgiveness. Having to both grant and accept forgiveness involving my husband, his ex-wife, and my stepchildren taught me that what I had leaned on in the past was not enough. I would not be able to get through these new situations without genuine forgiveness from my heart.

Discovering and practicing true forgiveness under these most difficult circumstances changed who I was. The seed was already there, but it blossomed in my stepfamily. I found that the need to grant and accept forgiveness was such a basic, core truth about me that I had to incorporate it into every aspect of my life. In just about every situation I face, my "forgiveness truth" is what I turn to first, before I make any decisions. That order of things simplifies my life.

The great benefit of learning this truth is that I can put things behind me more quickly. Now, when I get upset about something that my husband says or does, I don't waste a lot of time judging him or reliving the event. Instead of spending days arguing with him, I can move on. Honoring my truth helps me to let go of anger or frustration and look for ways to deal with an issue that will move us forward, not back.

Now it's your turn. Write a short paragraph about who you are and what defines you to others. Jot down the first answers that come to mind, as if you were talking with a friend over a cup of coffee. I've made you a handy fill-in-the-blank form to get you started:

I'm a woman who loves _____ and _____ and _____. I believe in _____ and _____. I find great enjoyment in _____and _____. I cannot tolerate _____ and _____. I am _____ and _____ and _____. I want to improve _____. More than anything, I want _____ and _____.

So, were you able to fill in the blanks completely, without breaking a sweat? If not, you soon will, because living in a stepfamily, you'll come to rely more and more on who you really are. You'll continually deepen what you know about yourself as you grow in your role. You may have to study and wrestle and work hard for quite a while to discover the deepest truths about yourself, but this paragraph is a good start.

Your core truths will become apparent if you keep looking for them. This quest is crucial to your communication with your family, because if you don't know who you are or don't present it well, you can't expect others to know either. You will have plenty of chances to show your family who you are, and many opportunities to work on improving your communication with them, because your communication challenges are there every day. Knowing your truths provides the clarity that leads to consistency. When your words reflect your truths, consistent communication will naturally follow.

Earlier, we talked about basing your actions on their relationship to your goals. The question there was: *Does this get me closer to my goal?* Here, the question that will guide you is: *Is this communication clear and consistent with who I am?* If it's not, you're complicating your life instead of simplifying it. That's a big mistake.

The question is simple. When you know who you are, the answer is simple, too. When you know who you are, you have your innermost truths to sustain you, to anchor you in the most troubling of times. When you know who you are, you bring a calming strength to your difficulties.

When you communicate in a compassionate way, consistent with your truths, your focus is clear. You know how to present your point of view and how to listen to someone else's. Since everyone knows where you stand, you can get straight to work on finding solutions. Fewer complications mean better communication.

In a family where change is the only constant, simplify what is in your control. You must communicate to grow, to reach the goal of a happy family. Make your part in that effort easier and more effective.

Learning how

I know that it sounds like you're the only one doing any work here! It's true that you can't control your family's reactions, or their communication habits. But you can control yours, and that alone will have a profound impact on your life. Here are some ways that you can learn what works for you and your family:

1. *Learn from yourself.* Pay attention to how you feel when you're trying to communicate with someone. Any discomfort you feel may come from the person you're dealing with. Though you can't make him or her change or just disappear, those feelings will teach you about yourself. They're there for a reason. They are telling you that the way you're communicating is not consistent with who you are.

Likewise, when the feelings inside you are comfortable ones, they're telling you that you are being true to who you are. That also means that you're communicating effectively. When your communication feels comfortable, there are fewer complications. Pay attention to that barometer in the pit of your stomach, because it's trying to tell you something.

Here's an example. If your husband frequently asks you to take care of his kids in his absence, and you always say "yes" to please him, even when you feel infringed upon, you're going to feel resentment and frustration, leading to a breakdown in communication between the two of you and ultimately a great big fight. If, on the other hand, you are able to say "no" (or even "yes, but . . ."), you can compassionately explain the reasons for your answer and look for understanding. With this approach, you're being true to yourself and honest with your husband. It's effective communication without the fight.

Tales from the Blender

When we first got married, I wasn't really an equal partner with my husband when it came to raising my stepdaughter. I was expected to assume all the responsibility of taking care of her, yet on many occasions I wasn't included in solving problems or dealing with issues. My opinion didn't count.

I often felt like an outsider in my own home, and began to feel anger and resentment toward my husband and stepdaughter whenever she would come to visit. As a stepmom friend said to me, "It's a horrible feeling to hear the door open and realize that you are about to become the least important person in the house."

I began to question whether I was being selfish or just plain mean. My best response was to say, "The percentage of my responsibility is equal to the amount of decision-making power that you instill in me." I finally had to detach, which I have been doing over the past four months. It was a struggle with my husband to set these boundaries, but there is peace in our house once again.

— *P.H., Orlando, Florida*

2. Learn from the past. When poor communication decisions have led to more confusion than growth, remember that confusion. And when you've had the foresight to choose wisely and your communication has led to understanding, remember that result, too. Build on the steps you've taken, both forward and backward, as you work to simplify your communication.

One of the areas where stepmoms and their husbands often find themselves at odds, for example, is in their parenting styles. What one considers acceptable, the other may find intolerable. You'll need to blend your styles for effective parenting, and you'll need to start with effective communication. If you cruelly attack your husband about his parenting decisions, you're not being compassionate. If you change your own style on a whim, you're not being consistent. Either way, the result is a problem on top of a problem: anger and resentment over your efforts to discuss your anger and resentment about your parenting styles.

When that happens, learn from it, as much as it hurts. Better communication choices, based on honesty and compassion, will lead to better understanding and a better chance for a solution.

Tales from the Blender

I think the word "compromise" is the single most important word in our vocabulary right now, and it *is* a struggle. My husband

and I each have to constantly remind ourselves that the other person is coming from a completely different set of expectations, and just because we disagree about a particular issue, it does not necessarily mean that either one of us is *wrong*. We just disagree.

We have to work together and communicate with each other about what's most important to each of us so that we can find some common ground. It is not easy. The goal is to ultimately end up in a place in which we all feel that we've gained something by forming this new family—hopefully, that we've gained more than we've lost.

— *Debbie Budesky, Marshall, Michigan*

Where it leads

Your communication problems didn't all appear overnight, and they won't be solved overnight. Give yourself and your family time to learn how to become better communicators. As you travel this bumpy road, full of potholes and debris, go slowly. Don't expect spontaneous and uninterrupted perfect communication among everyone—ever. You're not robots.

What you can expect, though, is improved communication, regardless of the effort anyone else makes, because of the effort *you're* about to make. Be true to yourself. Relate who you are to your family with honesty, compassion, and consistency. The result will be an enormous burden lifted from you. And that will lead to progress toward your goals and more peace and serenity for yourself and those around you.

Tales from the Blender

From the start of my marriage, I spent most of my time running my three stepkids around to different sports practices and activities. After about a year and a half of this, I was beginning to feel like a taxi service, maid, cook, waitress, and overall slave. To the kids, it was normal. They were starting to treat me like a mother. But never having been a mother, I didn't recognize it. Instead, I was feeling used and resentful. I was having a hard time communicating with them, and we were at odds most of the time.

One day, after I had been exceptionally crabby, I decided to put a note in each of their lunches to let them know that I did care about them, even if I didn't always act like it. Since then, I've been writing notes on their napkins at least a couple of times a week. It's just simple little things like "Have a nice day!" or "Good luck on your test today!" or my stepdaughter's favorite, "Happy Peanut Butter and Jelly Day."

I was surprised at how much that opened up the lines of communication. They suddenly saw me as someone they could talk to, and not just someone who was there to take care of the house and feed them. The more they opened up to me, the more I opened up to them, and we're all a little closer now.

— *Brenda, Ohio, stepmom of three*

———————————

CHAPTER 6

Simplify Your Authority

Power that touches with love is power that endures.

Do your stepchildren do everything you tell them to do, as soon as you ask? Do they respond with gratitude to the limits you set and embrace you when you deny them something they want? They don't? It sounds like they're fairly normal kids. Does their behavior make you want to pull your hair out or threaten to run away? Then you must be a fairly normal stepmom, too!

Shakespeare wrote that some people are born great, some achieve greatness, and some have greatness thrust upon them. That last part may be a pretty fair description of your position in the eyes of your stepchildren. To them, you certainly weren't born to greatness. In fact, you may not be very impressive to them at all, but you are an adult in their lives and that means that authority, if not greatness, has been thrust upon you.

That responsibility can blow up like a powder keg if you don't handle it carefully. Don't complicate or abuse your authority—just simplify it. That will bring great rewards for you and your stepchildren.

What is authority?

As a stepparent, like any other parent, one of your jobs is to provide structure for the children. That's what authority is all about: structure, not ambiguity; discipline, not fear. Kids—especially kids who have been through major family upheavals—need to know the rules of the game, and they are looking to you and their dad to provide them. Your united front is a critical part of your family structure. The kids need boundaries; you and your husband need the courage to supply them, working as a team, with both of you equally in charge.

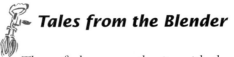 **Tales from the Blender**

The wife has no authority with the stepkids other than what her husband gives her. He has to demand their respect and good behavior. It's essential that he back her 100% in the kids' eyes. The couple needs to discuss this *before* the marriage. She needs to know what *he* sees as her role. If he expects her to

be an instant mom, he will be setting her up
for failure.

— *Polly Bywater, Tulsa, Oklahoma, mom
of four, stepmom of five, custodial of two*

Do not marry a man who does not know
how to discipline his children. Insist on a
united front when confronting, disciplining,
or making rules in your home. If he cannot
back you up and follow through, he is not
ready to be married.

— *Kathi O., stepmom and mom-to-be*

Authority is a crucial strand in the bonds between you
and your stepkids. Of course you want them to mind you and
behave well and clean up their rooms and do everything else
they should do to make your life easier. But *real* discipline
and authority are not only about changing behavior or taking
away a privilege when someone breaks the rules. They're about
teaching right from wrong, order from disorder, responsibility from indifference.

Exercising authority over your kids—all of them—means
to love them. When you welcome and accept that challenge
with your stepchildren, it means that you've chosen to love
them by disciplining them. The reasons behind your actions
are clear. It not only simplifies *your* life, it simplifies *theirs*,
too.

Establishing your authority as the stepmom may be relatively painless at times. At others, it may be the emotional equivalent of running head first into a wall. . . repeatedly. . . for about a year. Whatever the situation, you have the power to make choices that will help you. We'll talk about how in just a bit.

A *stepmom's authority*

You already know how to exercise your authority over your own children, if you have them. They have known for as long as they can remember that discipline is one way that you show your love for them. It's not an issue. But you may have to start from scratch with your stepchildren. Doing what you've done before may not work now, making you feel lost and unsure of your next turn.

When you are trying to accomplish so much so quickly for your family, finding ways to assert authority over your stepchildren may seem like one more problem that you'd rather avoid. But if you hide from it, you'll do both your stepchildren and yourself a disservice. It takes great courage to exercise your authority, but since it's an exercise of your love, you can't give up.

Even if it seems elusive or uncomfortable, you have both the right and the responsibility to enforce your authority. You don't have to ask for it or earn it or steal it. Realize that although this duty has been "thrust upon" you, you can choose to simplify it. Build your authority just as you do everything else—by remembering your goals and making good choices.

Enforcing your authority won't be the easiest thing you'll do, but simplifying it will pave the way for a happier, healthier family. A simplified authority will move you closer to a goal of a stronger stepfamily, because authority is about much more than correcting misbehavior. It's about building *trust*.

It's possible that your stepkids will comply with your requests early on, out of respect or deference to you as an adult or because their dad told them to. More likely, though, they won't truly acknowledge your authority until they know that you exercise it out of love and a sincere desire to take care of them. Only then will they realize that you are someone who cares and who is intimately involved in their lives. That will take time, but it's possible to make progress toward that goal right away.

But don't make your stepchildren figure it all out by themselves. They're a captive audience and you have the floor, so go ahead and make the first move. Don't be subtle. When your stepson grumbles about one of your decisions, look straight at him and say, in whatever words are appropriate to the situation and his age: "I'm doing this because I love you and I care about what happens to you. That's more important than whether or not you're happy with this choice. End of discussion."

And then tell yourself that the look on his face is not one of total disgust, just disguised amusement.

The value of rules

Establishing rules and structure for your home is a giant step toward simplifying your authority as a stepmom. Everybody in your new family is learning the chain of command, and you and your husband can make it easier with well-defined rules and expectations of behavior. When the two of you establish order in your home, you take the guesswork out of it. You make all of your lives easier.

Your house rules support your authority in these three ways:

1. They are a **roadmap** for the choices you have to make every day. Rules form a foundation that helps to make your choices simpler. You don't have to explain everything anew, a thousand times a day. You don't have to wonder what your husband would say. Instead, you can refer to what is already there. When you say, "No, you may not watch TV until your homework is done," or "Our limit on phone calls is thirty minutes, so you need to hang up now," you're not making it up as you go. The decisions are already made for you.

2. Your rules, and the reasons for them, are **easily defined**, so that everyone can understand them. They do a lot of work for you. Like speed limit signs and traffic signals, they become part of the scenery, and they are impartial. A "no eating in the living room" rule is easy to enforce with every child in your home. Your rules are a way to show your love for your stepchildren by making choices for their good. They'll eventually see that, too.

3. Rules bring **logic** to emotional situations, providing the detached clarity and stability you need in a heated mo-

ment. They come with reasons and consequences that are already established, and that's especially welcome in the emotional minefield that discipline can be. In a highly-charged interchange between you and your stepkids, a simple cause-and-effect explanation can be your best, least painful choice.

Tales from the Blender

My biggest mistake was in not *firmly* establishing some ground rules in the beginning, both with my husband and stepson. My husband is very permissive, while I'm from a structured background, and was always provided privacy and clear family rules. I've recommended to women contemplating marrying a guy with kids to make certain they both are very clear beforehand that they will be a united front with the children on all issues.

— *Cindy L., Nashville, Tennessee*

I am still struggling to establish authority over my stepson, not only because he hates the idea of having a stepmom, but because he doesn't seem to respect any authority and his mom and dad don't set clear boundaries for him. It's simply not acceptable for him to dribble ice cream on the computer keyboard, scatter toys everywhere, or smash food into the carpet, but my husband practically ignores these behaviors. He does support me when I make decisions and set rules, but it's exhausting to always have to be the bad guy. I've told him we need to set some house rules together, but he isn't interested!

Strangely, my stepson doesn't seem to have a problem with my direction and he usually does what I ask without question. I sometimes wonder whether he's testing me or if he honestly doesn't know what behaviors are proper, because they aren't modeled for him at home. I know that my husband just wants their limited time together to be special, happy, and fun—not full of rules, regulations, and conflicts. I wish I could make him understand that children need limits and boundaries, and that he's not doing his son any favors by being his buddy all the time instead of his parent.

— *S.S., Colorado*

Where to start

The first step in developing a structure is to spend some time with your husband discussing the vision you both have for your family. When you develop a vision together, you give your new life the well-defined beginning it deserves. Your vision will be what you and your husband most believe in and want to impart to your children. Respect, honesty, responsibility—these are the kinds of values that your vision must reflect. Be sure that the vision is one that the kids can easily grasp and adopt as their own.

Once you have agreed on your vision for your family, you will be able to develop rules that reflect it. Your rules will carry out your vision on a more tangible level. They are a joint effort between the two of you, designed to give all of your kids the best place to learn and grow, within the limits you've set. Rules, and the structure that you provide, will bring your vision of your family into clearer focus for each family member, every day.

Naturally, your rules will reflect your and your husband's value systems and personal goals. There are, however, some rules that are fairly consistent from stepfamily to stepfamily. These include:

❖ **Respect is paramount, between all adults and all children.** You can't decree that children love their stepparents, or that stepsiblings get along instantly, but you can demand that children treat everyone else in the family with respect. You must respect your stepchildren and their other family, too. They're all part of your life now.

❖ **Both parents can expect obedience from every child, regardless of biology.** The parents, whether they are the child's birth parent or stepparent, are in charge. Even if the kids don't want to accept the idea of submitting to an adult who isn't Mom or Dad, they are expected to respect the authority of their stepparent, just as they respect the authority of their own parent.

❖ **The rules of your house aren't better or worse that the rules in their other homes. They simply may be different.** You're not trying to have "better" rules than their other parent may have. You're just establishing the rules that work in *your* home, and those are independent of any other rules. Don't worry about conflicts between behavior codes. The kids will adapt quickly to different sets of expectations and guidelines, as long as they know what they are. If you don't treat this as a major issue, neither will the kids.

Perhaps you and your husband talked about rules for your home even before you married. Pre-planning is always helpful. But even if you did agree on some rules before you needed them, you've probably discovered some situations that never occurred to you, or that don't fit the expectations you had. Kids do have a way of keeping us surprised. Though you may have to adjust or amend the rules, you're starting out with a good foundation, based on the vision you've established for your family.

Some new stepparents, however, feel that they don't need to bother with a set of rules for their home. They think they can just combine "his" rules with "her" rules and the children will miraculously know what to do. That's a dangerous assumption. Making the children guess how their new family will operate is not only unproductive, it's unfair to everyone. The interactions among all of you are going to be more confusing than the tax code for a while. The kids—and the parents—need the new family to have a structure of its own.

As you create your rules, remember that less is more. Kids' attention spans are notoriously short, and they learn best a little at a time. They also respond better to fewer rules, consistently enforced, than to many rules, routinely overlooked. Stay focused on the issues that you want to make a priority in your household. Tackle the biggest issues first and paint with broad strokes. Fine-tune the rules as all of you adapt to your new family. You'll quickly see where more or less control is needed.

You may feel it's a burden to establish rules up front, but I encourage you to take the time to do it well. The rules you make today will provide you with quick, effective answers that will simplify every day that follows. Making your house rules clear is the first step toward simplifying your authority. Don't underestimate the power of rules. They provide the structure that will grow your kids and simplify your days.

Tales from the Blender

What we have had to do to regain control is simply say, "This is our house and these are our rules. When you go to Mom's house or Grandma's or other relatives', I can't control what happens there. In our house, this is what we believe, these are our rules, and they won't change."

—*Isabella, New York*

My stepdaughter requires a lot of attention, due to her hectic schedule of being bounced back and forth each day. She gets no discipline at her mother's house. So I feel we have to teach and discipline harder at our house. She also tries to play my husband and me against each other. He tends to let her get away with more than I would. If I say something, she will go whine to him. But now we play as a team. Whatever he says, I agree with and whatever I say, he agrees with. Discipline is hard.

— *Michele, stepmom of one*

Informing the masses

Effective rules must be clear to everyone involved. Some stepparents call a family meeting to announce their rules. This especially helps when the children's behavior is a long way from where the parents believe it should be. If that approach seems to be what you need, do it in a fun, positive way that tells the children, "We're establishing some order in our home so that everyone knows the rules, and so that we can all be happier." Don't expect them to be delighted by your edict, but don't let them sway you from it, either.

Rules, of course, are worthless unless there are consequences for breaking them. Outline what will happen when they break the rules. They will think of it as punishment; you will explain it as free will. You've given them the rules and if they choose to break them, they will have to deal with what comes next. Convince them that any consequences they may face are up to them. You may as well teach them now that they can simplify their lives by making good choices!

Even after you've established rules for your home and have explained them fully, you can't control what happens next. It has been ordained from above since the dawn of time: Kids will bend or break rules on occasion, no matter who set them. Don't take it personally—it's their job. Just keep doing yours. Follow through with the consequences, look on their transgressions as learning experiences, and think of the whole process as a unique form of "quality time."

Remember that your family is a benevolent dictatorship. You decide what's best for your subjects, in this case, the children. They may not equate discipline with love as quickly as you do (they'll probably focus more on the "dictatorship" than the "benevolent"), so keep reminding them that the rules are for everyone's benefit. Tell them that as often as it takes, until they feel it in their hearts.

As mentioned earlier, many stepchildren will believe at first that the rules that apply at one home automatically apply at the other parent's house as well. That may be the case, and it may not. If your standards of behavior are poles apart from those of the other parents, the transition between homes can be very difficult. Acknowledge that there can be different rules for different homes, and say that while you won't try to control what they do elsewhere, you and their dad are in control of *your* home. Bless their quick little minds, kids easily learn what they can get away with and what they can't, *if* the information is clear and the consequences are consistent.

The structure that you and your husband provide will set the tone for your home, one of unity and logic: "We love you and this is one way we're showing it." Keep in mind that just like you, the kids are struggling to reconcile all of the changes they've been through. Expect some resentment and lack of cooperation, and take comfort in knowing that most families, even traditional ones, experience the same thing, especially during the teen years. The strong structure you have created gives the kids something to grasp, a foundation on which to build their new life.

Tales from the Blender

My stepdaughters apparently had been raised by wolves. These pre-teen girls didn't even own toothbrushes the first time they spent the night at my house! They threw candy wrappers on the living room floor, helped themselves to my personal things, had the worst table manners I have ever seen, and constantly argued with me and their father. They had absolutely no respect for anyone or anything.

It was so bad some weekends that I threw them *all* out of my house, hoping they would never return. We took them on vacation with us after we were married, and it was an absolute disaster. When we returned, I announced that they were not welcome in our home, and for

several months my husband visited them elsewhere. Although I felt in control of my life again,
I also felt guilty. I had made him choose between his girls and me, and he had chosen me.

I began to join them for some of their din-
ners out. My husband apparently had been
working on them. The girls finally understood
that I meant what I said, and that they had
pushed me too far. They began to watch their
behavior around me. Eventually, I allowed
them to come over for an afternoon. It went
well. After several visits, I allowed them to
spend the night. We have progressed back to
every other weekend and I enjoy seeing them.

I had told them that when their behavior
was decent they would feel better about themselves and they would begin to build self-es-
teem. They do and they are. I really think it
was a matter of holding firm to my expectations. These kids had never been presented
with boundaries.

— *Judy*

Toward the goal of simplified authority

Showing love and concern for your stepkids may be difficult at times, especially if they are fighting you at every turn. It's hard to maintain your focus when you're in the trenches, battling behavior that requires you to enforce the rules. You have to do *something*, and you want it to be right. The question to ask yourself when deciding how to respond is: *does this choice show my love and give them the structure and discipline they need?* Answer and proceed accordingly, every time.

For example, if your stepdaughter has acted aggressively toward another child, you'll have to decide what to do. Ignoring the behavior might be the least painful choice, but that won't help her grow and learn. Nor will it show that you have her best interests at heart. The better response means more work, but it also means that you care.

When you discipline a stepchild for misbehavior, tell him or her why you are doing it. Be sure to do the same with your own children. Kids generalize very well. When your stepchildren see you use the same reasoning with your children and understand that they, too, will face unpleasant consequences at times, your stepchildren will be even more convinced of your love for them. Although these situations may not seem important at the time, they build on each other and get you closer to your goal.

Providing discipline is a touchy but necessary part of your job description. Make no mistake: as with your other efforts, your work here is continuous, constantly waxing and waning to meet the demands of the moment. The children will resist you from time to time. They can't help it, but you can make it work by approaching it in a simple way. Here are a few recommendations to help you get a handle on this messy issue of authority:

1. Start slowly. The transition from divorced and single-parent homes to combined homes with stepparents and stepsiblings makes running NATO look easy. Kids want to hold on to the familiar, and may view learning a new set of rules as just another imposition. Meanwhile, everyone is trying to get to know everyone else—their thoughts and habits and expectations—without the benefit of traditional family ties, and often on a part-time basis. Relax. Give them time. Take the pressure off everyone, including yourself. Realize that you won't be able to exercise authority with grace and finesse immediately. Nor will you make the right choice in every discipline decision right away. (Actually, you won't *ever* be able to make the right choice every time, but you *will* get infinitely better at it.)

Don't expect conformity the instant you're all gathered under the same roof. You'll sometimes be surprised by what elicits a negative reaction. When that happens, remember that discipline is love. If you and your stepchild haven't yet built the relationship you want, remember to say up front, every time, that you love him or her, and that's why you're making this choice. That is always your best comeback when a child fights a decision you've made. Point out that you're being consistent with the rules of the house. Then leave it alone. Don't worry if he or she doesn't embrace your logic right then. Children often hear and remember far more than we give them credit for.

Ease into your authority role as quietly as possible. Save the biggest issues for their father to handle alone at first.

Everyone is trying to find their place in the new family and many of the early discipline problems will reflect that uncertainty and confusion. Don't add to the problems by trying too hard, too fast. There's plenty of time. Take it slow.

Tales from the Blender

My biggest mistake as a stepmom was to assume too much parental responsibility too fast. I like things kept orderly and done properly. Suddenly having three children who don't like things orderly and have never been expected to do things properly drove me crazy.

It took me a while to understand that I couldn't expect the kids to be perfect, and that my yelling and nagging wasn't motivating them. It also was not my job to discipline the children, especially when my husband was there. It was a mistake to let that happen. I came to realize that some things are just not as important as I thought. I have to make a conscious effort to determine if what I am about to get upset over is really worth it. It's an ongoing process of re-training myself.

— *Brenda, Ohio, stepmom of three*

2. Assume authority as the parent. This may sound like a contradiction of what I just said, but let me explain. As we've said, you have both the right and the obligation to discipline your stepchildren, providing them with boundaries that give them a safe place to grow. Start slowly, yes, but be very clear about your position.

Many stepmoms are all too familiar with the cry of the belligerent, unruly stepchild: "You're not my mother!" The truth is, you're not. So agree with them, and then offer the classic stepmother reply: "I'm the mother in *this* house. We have our own rules and you'll follow them." Then move on.

You are the stepmom, neither a tyrant nor a doormat. You're the adult, you're in charge, and you have the power to enforce the rules of your home. Explain your reasoning as clearly as you can, sticking to the facts of the situation, rather than how angry or appalled you are by your stepchild's behavior. You enforce your rules because you can, and because it's the right thing to do.

3. Invest some time up front. I bet it sounds like I'm recommending that you add a complication to your life. Well, it probably *will* be a bit more complicated for a while, but spending time on power struggles early on will greatly simplify the situations that follow.

Kids love to test ultimatums, and your stepkids will be no exception. This is what happens: You ask your stepson to do this or that, adding that if he doesn't, something he won't enjoy will happen. He doesn't believe you and calls your bluff. Now you have a decision to make. You can take the easy way out by not following through with the consequences. In choosing that option, you fail to do your job of providing the discipline your stepson needs. Or you can view the situation as an opportunity to build courage. That means taking a deep breath and applying the consequences, which you know he will find unpleasant. By investing your time and energy right then, you will simplify the next situation that arises.

I'll give you an example. My son learned as a very young child that when he didn't do what he was told, he'd have to deal with the consequences. Even though following through was often the most tiring, not-fun thing for me to do, I did it anyway, because I wanted him to understand the rules and limits I had provided for him. I felt that I always acted out of love and my duty to teach him valuable life lessons.

Ever the over-achiever, I believed it was my duty to also teach these lessons to my stepsons, even if it killed us. The first horrible showdown almost did.

It was just a normal evening, probably a year or so into my life as a stepmom. My younger stepson, age nine at the time, had been playing with some toy motorcycles on the living room floor. It was getting late, and I told him to carry the toys upstairs the next time he went. If he left them on the floor, I warned, they'd be mine.

Naturally, he left the motorcycles sitting there. I picked them up and put them in a kitchen cabinet. A little while later, he came looking for his toys. "I told you not to leave them down here, or I'd get them," I told him. "You know the rules. You can have them back tomorrow." I expected that after a few pleading requests, he'd go on to something else.

Boy, did I miss that one. The begging and whining and crying went on for *hours*. My husband was at work, and I wouldn't let my stepson call him. This showdown was strictly between this little boy and me.

I did my best to explain my logic. "If I give the toys back to you now, after all this whining, you'll just whine longer next time." He disagreed, but I was unmovable. I realized that although our relationship was normally warm and caring, we had reached a pivotal point. Or maybe both of us were just having a very, *very* bad day. Still, I had taken a position and I was going to stick with it.

He knew that I had the authority to enforce our house rules on my own. I also had a responsibility to myself to simplify that authority by following through on the consequences. Was that part simple? Hardly. It was one of the hardest things I've ever done. I had to be willing to sacrifice something *now* (his approval) for what he needed for the *future* (structure and security). God, it hurt. But I had made my stand, and it was time to put up or shut up.

After I had crawled into bed, crying, my heart pounding, feeling worse than I had felt in a long time, I heard my stepson coming down the stairs. He walked into my room, red-eyed and exhausted.

"I'm sorry," he said.

"I'm sorry, too, baby," I told him. "Do you understand–?" I tried to ask.

"I understand," he said.

I held him to me. "I love you so much. Since Dad's working, why don't you lay down in here with me for a while, okay?"

"I love you, too," he said.

He crawled into bed with me and we laid there, both of us exhausted and thankful that the horror show was over. We've never talked about it or relived it. We don't need to.

4. Use proactive authority. Wow, that sounds impressive, doesn't it? It's not, really. All it means is to develop the habit of paying attention so that you can head off problems before they get out of hand. This habit grows over time as you get to know your stepchildren better and know what to expect in certain situations.

For example, your stepkids may need a little while to fully adjust to your rules after they've been at their other home. It's not an identity crisis; it's just part of the fallout from being members of two primary families. Be prepared for that, and allow everyone time to get back on the same page of the rulebook, so to speak. Avoid trouble spots and save important announcements or decisions until everyone feels more connected.

Tales from the Blender

By providing a structured environment for my husband's children every time they visit (ten to twelve days a month), anxieties are lowered, because we all know pretty much what to expect. For example, the kids know they're expected to put their overnight bags up in their rooms when they first arrive, instead of leaving them strewn about the office or living room. Then we all have an after-dinner snack or play outside, weather permitting. We have set weeknight and weekend bed-

times, as well as wake-up times. The kids also
have age-appropriate chores, something they
do not have at their mother's house, to the
best of our knowledge.

— *Kelly, stepmom of three, Connecticut*

After a while, you'll be able to anticipate the situations
that may trigger discipline problems, and you can enlist your
husband's help before they happen. If he can't be there to
support you, get his opinion beforehand, so you can offer it
when the kids ask. It's not that you need his approval, since
you've already established your house rules together. You're
merely simplifying difficult situations by putting some thought
into them before they even occur. Having the answers before
the questions are asked is always a great plan, not to mention
a surprise to those around you. You can have a few tricks up
your sleeve now and then, too.

Are you amazed by the many hidden talents that you've
discovered since becoming a stepmom? When the children's
security and best interests are at stake, I know that you'll
choose the simple, effective approach every time.

The best benefit

If you've been having a difficult time disciplining your
stepchildren, you may be more interested in abandoning your
authority than working to simplify it. Don't give up. The most

wonderful benefit of simplifying your authority is a truly serendipitous prize, one that is worth all of the work. What you'll win is the *trust* of your stepchildren, and that doesn't come cheaply.

Stepchildren, perhaps more than other children, are looking for something solid, something that isn't going to change. They are looking for security, and the adults in their lives can provide that by being consistent. When you follow through with what you promise—consistently and completely, even when the kids complain about the consequences—they learn to trust you in other areas as well. They learn that they can count on your word.

Never forget that discipline is love. Sooner or later your stepchildren will see that, if you make it simple enough for them. Children thrive on repetition. Use that to your advantage, and keep showing them, even when it's hard on you both, that you are exercising your authority out of love for them. When you make an unpopular choice because it's the right thing to do, your stepchildren will trust you to do your best for them in *all* circumstances. Embrace their trust. You've earned it.

Tales from the Blender

One day, I kissed my fiancé goodbye as he dropped me off, but forgot to kiss my 4-1/2 year-old stepson like I usually do. A moment later, as I was opening the door to my building, I heard an insistent honking. I turned to see my fiancé waving at me from the car. I came over and saw my stepson looking quite upset. I asked him what was wrong. He said, pouting, "You did not kiss *me* goodbye!" My heart just melted. I took him in my arms and gave him a warm hug and a sweet kiss. I told him I loved him with all my heart. This was truly my happiest moment as a stepmom, one that I will forever cherish.

— *Jessy V.-H., Berkeley, California*

CHAPTER 7

Simplify Your Future

The best is yet to be, but I'll grab my blessings now, too.

Sometimes you have a day that's just great. You know the ones I mean, those times when your maternal instincts are graciously rewarded, love is in bloom, and everyone you know is happily pursuing their own life, leaving you to pursue yours. The world is one big picnic, and looks as if reaching your goals is going to be child's play. You start to think that tomorrow couldn't possibly be better than today.

Days like that do happen from time to time, though they can fade from your memory as easily as some obscure fact about the Revolutionary War. I'll wager that having a bunch of those days is at the top of your wish list. When everything comes together, you can see, even if just briefly, that your efforts are worth it.

It should be simple to have more of those magical days—and it can be. Do your part to simplify your future. Do your best to bring about more perfect days.

When you do everything we've talked about to simplify your present, you're simplifying your future as well. It happens automatically. Everything you do today that is positive and focused on your goals cannot help but simplify your future.

Remember that when the complications of your life pile up too quickly. Remember that when you search in the mirror for the part of you that is strong enough and courageous enough to handle the challenges of this life. Remember that when you have to stop, slow down, focus, and clarify before you can move forward. Remember all of that, and make the choice to simplify your future.

I'll show you three ways to get started.

One: Become a collector

All stepmoms become great collectors. It's something that we do at first for the surprising joy of it and then forever after for survival. Since our world is full of complications and traumas, doubts and fears, our place in it is more secure when we take the time to acknowledge the good that also happens in our lives. We simplify our future when we collect from the past and present.

The things that stepmoms collect aren't found in any store or online auction. But when you begin to pay attention, you'll be amazed to realize how many of these "collectibles" are hidden in the daily grind. Don't overlook them. They will surprise and overpower you. You will find great strength and peace in those times when you can see a little bit of heaven peeking through the clouds.

I'll give you an example, one that seems like such a little thing.

It was a nothing-out-of-the-ordinary weekend afternoon. My younger stepson was at the kitchen table, piling a plate high with what undoubtedly was not a very nutritious snack. I was there too, wiping up his mess.

"What day is today?" he asked absentmindedly.

"Saturday," I said, as I dusted potato chip and cookie crumbs into the trash can. "What day did you want it to be?"

"Saturday," he repeated. "That's good. I didn't want it to be Sunday." With that, he swooped up his plate and headed to the living room, without realizing what he had just done for me.

My memory-grabbing antennae had shot up when I heard his comment. This one was a keeper. I stopped my progress with the dishcloth and said a prayer of thanks. I didn't want it to be Sunday, either, because then he'd be leaving for his mom's house.

My stepson's comment was a breath of peace and joy. It was hope and redemption. It was a good moment that put many difficult ones into perspective. It helped me simplify my future because it showed me that something very good was happening in the life we were building with these kids. It was a tiny step toward my goal. I could let go of some of my worry and fear because, at least every now and then, I could see that we were on the right track.

For him, it was a meaningless exchange, one that I'm sure he doesn't even remember. To me, it was much more. Thankfully, I was paying attention.

Those kinds of moments are meant to be collected. Take them whenever you can find them. They will sustain you when you don't know if you can go on. Find the good and positive points in every situation, even when things don't go exactly the way you've planned, and focus on those. Make special note of the times when you are more step*family* than *step*family, then hold on tightly at those other times when you feel you're losing faith. Take the best parts and build from there, always forward, never back.

Some collectible moments come upon you like a cloudburst, catching you unaware. These can linger in your thoughts, reminding you of what you have accomplished. That happened to me one night, when a total stranger saw something I had missed.

The five of us were together in a store, which is a little unusual since none of us is much of a shopper. We were looking for fabric to cover the video game chairs that my husband had made for the boys. After choosing the prints they wanted, the kids wandered over to the sporting goods department with my husband, while I waited to have the fabric cut. I hadn't paid much attention to the sales clerk until I dropped the bolts on the table.

"Three boys?" she asked as she unfurled the wildly-colored cloth.

I gave my most pitiable look, as if to say yes, they really do exasperate me sometimes!

"I have boys, too," she continued. "I always wanted a girl. I have a stepdaughter, but steps aren't the same. . . ." Her voice trailed off.

I just looked at her. I couldn't say a word.

By that time, she was double-checking my yardage and calculating prices. She handed me the cloth and said good night. I never had a chance to correct what she had assumed about my family.

For whatever reason, another stepmom had taken me for just a regular mom. She had seen something in our relationship that made her think that all of the boys were mine. Had we overcome so much that our progress was more visible than our failures? Had I taken all that we'd accomplished for granted? I don't know, but I've thought of that night often. I'm grateful that my stepsons and I have managed to build something real and lasting and really quite simple when we let it be, when we worry less about biology and concentrate more on the family we are today. And I'm grateful to a stranger for reminding me of it.

Look for those kinds of keepers in your life, too. File away every good exchange between you and your stepchildren and every special moment between you and your husband. Then reach for them when you need a boost. I keep a "special moments" journal to record happy and wonderful times I have with my husband. Some entries are only one line; some cover an entire weekend. They all are priceless, and they are just for me. They remind me of my ability to carry on when life gets really hard. They are a tremendous source of strength.

Start your own collection. You don't have to write down every moment of joy, but whatever you include will help you focus. It will be a reminder of what you're working toward and what you've accomplished so far. You'll be amazed how quickly you'll be able to add to it when you pay attention to what's happening around you, the wonderful amid the difficult.

Right here, start being a Great Collector. Note five "keeper moments" that have happened in your family. Then get yourself a notebook and continue the list. It's a simple but effective way to work on your goals, because these good memories will give you the strength and determination to continue in the face of hardship or failure.

My keepers:

1. _____

2. _____

3. _____

4. _____

5. _____

Tales from the Blender

It's the little things that tell me that they love me, such as:

❖ They want to wear one of my T-shirts to bed at night.

❖ They sit on my lap to watch TV and fall asleep there or in my arms.

❖ Mothers Day cards picked out by the child with no coaxing by Dad.

❖ They surprised me with breakfast by candlelight one morning for no reason!

❖ The little one wants to be a nurse just like me when she grows up.

❖ They say "I love you" in person and on the phone, even if their mom is present.

❖ They run to me after school with a big hug.

❖ They call me "Stepzilla" and laugh and laugh and say "you're not a mean step-mom." I gave myself that nickname to beat them to the punch. Now it is a term of endearment.

— *Kathi O., stepmom and mom-to-be*

❖ When my oldest stepdaughter (age 23) told me that she aspired to the kind of relationship her dad and I have.

❖ When my oldest stepson tells me he thinks I'm doing a great job.

❖ When my 16 year-old stepdaughter hugs me and tells me she loves me.

❖ When my 13 year-old stepdaughter says, "You're the greatest," just because I bought Pop-Tarts for her.

— *Polly Bywater, Tulsa, Oklahoma, mom of four, stepmom of five, custodial of two*

Two: Protect your marriage

It's truly bizarre that we marry the man we are meant to be with, only to nearly abandon him as we struggle with responsibilities that multiply like fruitcakes on Christmas Eve. We get so busy tending to other parts of our life that we put our marriages on hold while we fight the hottest fire. That approach is about as backward as you can get.

The one steady rock in the earthquake happening all around you is your marriage. Because it is the most important relationship you have, the condition of your marriage will dictate the condition of your future. That is not an overstatement. Protect your marriage, and you protect your future.

I gave you the sobering statistics before, but I'll tell you again: almost two-thirds of the re-marriages that include children fail. They don't fail just because they're complicated. They fail because they don't get the protection they need in a life that is filled with danger. Your marriage will not survive on its own. It will not become the world's greatest marriage just because you thought it would when you fell in love. It is not going to survive just because loss and pain have brought you together. It *can* survive, *in spite of* your history, but only if you protect it.

This marriage is more vulnerable that your first marriage or any other relationship. There is a lot more clutter around you—things like pettiness and jealousy and dishonesty. By ridding yourself of the clutter, you make your marriage stronger and guarantee it another day of life. When you learn how to protect your marriage, you simplify a future that without a doubt will be faced with threats from time to time.

The forces that threaten your marriage come from both inside and outside the walls of your home. From the outside, you may be threatened by a former spouse who won't let go or a job that separates you and your husband for long periods of time. Inside your home, there may be threats from bickering children, financial strain, or your own insecurity. I don't know which kind are more dangerous, but you simplify your future when you eliminate or at least minimize them.

Think about the forces that threaten your marriage. In the left-hand column below, list five threats to your marriage:

Threats to my marriage: Ways to simplify them:

1. _____   _____
2. _____   _____
3. _____   _____
4. _____   _____
5. _____   _____

Now consider what you can do to simplify each one. Why are these forces a threat? Are you partly responsible for allowing any of them to become a threat? Have you given them more power than they actually have? Are any of them just leftover clutter than needs to be swept away? How much control over each one do you truly have?

Next to each threat write one thing you can do today to simplify each one. That may be nothing more than making an effort to view the threat in a different way, or deciding to discuss it with your husband. These first steps are only a tiny start. Starting small is fine; just don't stop. No matter what step you take, it is powerful, because it signifies your willingness to take action to protect your marriage.

Your ability to deal with threats will improve as your strength and confidence in your marriage grows. But first, vow that you will put its survival before all else. The threats to your marriage may change over time, but they will never come to an end. Allow the forces that would destroy your marriage to get close and you'll shatter your chances of reaching your goals. Each one of them, in some way, depends on the health of your marriage. Let it die, and all of your goals die, too. Put your efforts and energies into protecting your marriage, and you'll have the foundation for reaching your goals.

Protecting and nurturing your marriage by putting it first simplifies your life, because your marriage should be a major source of your strength. You have chosen to have a future with your husband, a future that will include the two of you long after the children are grown and former spouses are just faded memories. You simplify that future now, today, when you recognize that protecting your marriage is essential to your goal of a happy, healthy family.

Three: Follow your heart

You now view your entire world through the prism of being a stepmom. It has become your life's breath and consumes your soul. It takes all of your concentration and devotion. It's hard work! But it's also the most amazing journey you'll ever take. Together, we've discovered how you can simplify it and achieve the kind of life you want.

Now, as we talk about your future, one that is defined by your family roles, take a moment to separate yourself from them. I know that sounds like I'm just complicating things again, but I promise that I'm not. Just bear with me for a moment.

In our work together, you've learned how to simplify many of the issues in your complex life. You've learned that there is a lot that you indeed can control. You've learned that clarity and focus will enable you to make the choices that will propel you toward your goals. You've learned who you are and how to grow your family. You've learned how to handle the difficult relationships in your life and how to communicate with compassion and consistency. You've learned how to discipline your stepkids with love. You've learned that your marriage is your lifeline.

Now simplify the rest of your future by learning how to make some other choices—the ones that are just about *you*. What is it, besides growing this family, that you need to do just for you? What is hidden there, in the private depths of your mind and heart, that you can't let go of? What do you want for *you*?

Yes, I know, things are already complicated and your days are already full. But this is something you can't ignore. You know that clarity and focus simplify your obligations as a stepmom. The same is true for goals that are just for you. Simplify your future by knowing where you're going. Don't ignore or delay the goals that are in your heart just because you're in one of the most complex kind of lives there is.

When the winds blow hard in your stormy life, there should be a wonderful place where you can feel powerful and strong and in control. Set aside a part of your life and create that place for yourself. In the middle of all the work you do for others, don't neglect the work that's just for you. You need and deserve to reach goals that are only about what *you* want to accomplish with your life.

What do you do just for yourself?

I usually don't feel right taking off alone when the kids are with us. So instead of shopping, going to the library, or getting a manicure (the things I usually do when I want to recharge my batteries), I often retreat to my bedroom to read. I keep the door open and I let my 10 year-old stepdaughter join me—if and only if she agrees to be quiet and read a book herself. I get some needed downtime and my stepdaughter and I get to spend time together.

— *Kelly, stepmom of three, Connecticut*

I pray lots and take time out for an occasional pedicure!

— *Ann, stepmom of one son*

I scrapbook! The kids are all deciding they want to scrapbook too, so it may turn out to be a family thing. Pretty cool to have your stepkids get into your hobby!

— *Angie, mom of two and stepmom of two*

I am Polish/Italian mix, so every so often I treat myself to one of the dishes I grew up on but my kids won't touch. I do cross-stitch, I read books, and in the spring months I garden. Sometimes I go for a walk if I feel mad, frustrated, or upset.

— *Isabella, New York*

I take yoga! Meditation is great!

— *A stepmom from Texas*

I work in my garden, which is very therapeutic. I also try and go to a ladies' Bible study. Prayer is very important.

— *Jenny, mom of one and stepmom of three*

When you have personal goals alongside your goals for your family, you have even more clarity and focus. When you know where you want to be and acknowledge how important it is to you to get there, you can take the next step, and then the one after that, and on and on, until you're there. By simplifying your family roles, using all the steps we've learned, you have more time and energy to spend on the goals that are just for you. Then you not only simplify your future, but you guarantee that it will be one you have chosen.

So listen carefully. Do you hear that indomitable voice from deep within you that wants so badly to be heard? What is it saying? Listen to it, and then write the top three goals that are just for you.

My goals for myself:

1. _____

2. _____

3. _____

Much of what we've learned about simplifying life in your stepfamily will help simplify your work toward your personal goals, too. Once again, it's about making choices and controlling what is yours to control. In the case of these personal goals, nearly all of the steps are within your control. Simplify your future by following your heart. Enjoy!

The unexpected rewards

My efforts at simplifying my life sometimes have been misunderstood. Too lazy to attend this meeting or that event, Karon? No, I profess, it's my choice not to go. Are you aware that your clothes are five years out of style? Yes, I know that.

I just haven't chosen to take the time to shop in a while. Sometimes they understand, and sometimes they don't.

Your efforts to simplify your life also may be misinterpreted at times, but that's okay. Just follow my lead and understand your actions for what they truly are—an appreciation of the simple and surprising joys of life. You can find them anywhere, if you're watching for them. I've even found some under a layer of dust.

I have to admit that I'm not the world's greatest housekeeper. I'll grab on to any excuse to get out of cooking and cleaning. I do throw away the garbage, and so manage to keep us from being condemned by the health department, and about once a month, I locate a mop—one that hasn't been turned into the checkered flag for a four-wheeler race—and actually use it on the floors.

But there is one item in my home that I absolutely never go anywhere near with a bottle of cleanser. Some might call it laziness; I call it the ability to recognize unexpected blessings when they find you.

I never wash my bathroom mirror.

This special mirror is an old picture frame, divided into four ten-by-twelve-inch panes, that we found on the side of the road. I painted it hunter green and filled each pane with a mirror. Originally it was merely functional, cheap, and convenient. Now it's become a memory.

One night, as I slapped back the shower curtain and stood dripping in the tub, already thinking about the next chore on my list, I glanced over at the mirror. There, drawn in the steam on the lower left pane, was a goofy monkey face with tiny ears and a big smile.

At first it felt like just one more thing that somebody had left for me to clean up, instead of hurrying out of the bathroom as I had commanded. My first inclination was to call the offending party back to clean it. (I was sure of who that was.) Then, in a moment of intense clarity and inspiration, I saw another possibility, the simple one. And I took it.

I stepped out of the shower and wrote "GOOD JOB!" under the monkey face in my clearest block letters. I wanted the message to be easy to read the next time my little graffiti artist took a bath.

I never said a word about it and didn't know how long I'd have to wait for a response. Finally, a few weeks later, I pushed the shower curtain back one evening, looked into the steamy mirror, and there it was—another drawing. The funny face in the lower right pane had fuzzy hair, big eyes, and another smile that reached across its face. I couldn't help smiling back at it. Again there was room underneath for a message. "BOO!" I wrote. Several more weeks passed and I couldn't wait any longer. One night, on the top left pane, I drew a funny face of my own. I tried to make it look like a girl by giving it longer hair, and I drew a big smile on her face. I left room for a message underneath. Every night, I looked for a response. Finally, there it was: "COOL!!" in childlike print. The timeless compliment.

There was only one pane left.

The last drawing looked like a Mr. Potato Head with spiked hair, big ears, and a smile the width of his face. There wasn't much room for my message. This would be the last one I could leave, so I thought hard about what to write. Then I decided not to write any words. I just drew three hearts underneath Mr. Potato Head. That seemed best.

Now, every time I step out of the shower amid the fog and steam, my thoughts aren't on household chores or the next decision I have to make. Instead, the first thing I see is the silent interaction between my stepson and me. It is a comfort and an inspiration. It brings a smile to my face and a warmth to my heart.

I know that they're just a few simple drawings etched in steam, but to me they're also proof that at least once I saw clearly enough to make the simple choice. I chose growth and possibility, hope and trust. The mirror stands today to remind me to slow down, to remember my goals, and to choose simplicity. That's always the best choice.

My housekeeping may improve as the kids get older and the craziness in my life subsides. It doesn't matter. I'll still never wash my bathroom mirror.

Tales from the Blender

When Mike and I got married, he and his 11 year-old came to live with my 13 year-old son and me. Saying it has been a challenge would be a gross understatement. The boys' sullen, disagreeable attitudes often resulted in a war of "us" versus "them."

How difficult it is to bond with an adolescent who I didn't know and love as a child!

My husband and I soon realized that we didn't have any memories of each other's sons when they were younger. So we took out some old Kinderfoto shots and shared pictures and stories of what the boys were like before they reached the age when everything parents do and say is embarrassing or stupid.

I told Mike about little redheaded Alex's adventure into a box of powdered sugar-covered donuts, taking a bite from each one and leaving a trail of white dust from his face to the floor. I heard about 3 year-old Jeff throwing a football back and forth while hamming it up for the camera. We've put some of the pictures around our home to help remind us of the days when the kids were just more fun to be around.

I'd like to say we're like the Brady Bunch now, but of course that's science fiction, not real life. Sometimes, though, those pictures and stories help us to laugh and put teenage antics into perspective. A sense of history, as well as a strong sense of humor, is a must in surviving a stepfamily.

— *Karen Ryan, Erie, Pennsylvania*

Afterword

There are few challenges that can be as formidable yet remarkable as succeeding as a stepmom and second wife. Being in a stepfamily will be your greatest heartache and your greatest joy. It can destroy you—or it can enrich and inspire you. It is one of life's most complicated family arrangements, filled with unnatural situations and complex relationships, but it is also one of life's most unbelievable bounties, presenting unique opportunities for learning, growing, and becoming. This is the life you have chosen. Take it and simplify it.

To manage the multiple demands of your life, you need only the courage to make simple choices. I know that as you struggle with the issues that are unique to steplife, you'll often question your approach and doubt your chances for success. But if you stay focused on your commitment to the marriage that brought you to this family, you'll get closer to your goals every day. Remember what you want from this life. As you collect your "special moments," be grateful for the progress you've made. Anticipate even more wonderful blessings.

I never tire of hearing my husband say how much he loves me, but he rarely waxes poetic about our life. Still, I do my best to get him to say the pretty things I want to hear.

Once, near our anniversary, I was hoping for at least a few complete sentences to the effect that he couldn't live without me. I kept prompting him with comments and open-ended questions about our past and our future. He mostly just agreed with whatever I said. Normally, I would have accepted that, but this time it wasn't enough for me.

Over lunch one day, I tried again. "It's hard to believe we've been married this long already. What do you think about when you think about that?" I figured that the answer to this question *had* to be long and elaborate. I hoped that the world would stand still while he professed his love and undying devotion to me.

He didn't even miss a bite of his egg salad sandwich.

"That's just how it is," he said, shrugging his shoulders. I may as well have asked his opinion on the change of seasons.

That's just how it is. His response wasn't eloquent or particularly romantic, but it was stunning in its power.

I was too dumbstruck to respond, but he didn't notice. He refilled his tea glass, dropped his paper plate in the trash, kissed me on the cheek, and went outside. I sat there and thought, he's right. That's just how it is. The two of us—together, confident, and determined to complete this mission. No doubts, no fears, no complications that we can't handle.

That's about as simple as it gets.

Bibliography

Listed alphabetically by title

Becoming Family: How to Build a Stepfamily That Really Works by Robert H. Lauer, Ph.D., and Jeanette C. Lauer, Ph.D. (Augsburg Fortress, 1999)

Written from a Christian perspective, this book is extremely well-organized and packed with concrete, real-life guidance. The chapters stress the importance of seeing each family member's point of view and give practical, easy to understand advice that focuses on strengthening the marriage and new family bonds. **Best:** The Ex-Factor—dealing with the challenges of a former spouse.

Blended Families: Creating Harmony As You Build a New Home Life by Maxine Marsolini (Moody Press, 2000)

This book begins with the author's heartbreaking personal story and includes several examples of the challenges other stepfamilies have faced. Relying heavily on Christian principles, it offers inspiring and helpful suggestions. The author covers attitudes, money matters, and more, and includes a chapter on "making the best of it." **Best:** The end-of-chapter "Growth and Application" questions.

Blending Families: A Guide for Parents, Stepparents, Grandparents and Everyone Else Building a Successful New Family by Elaine Fantle Shimberg (Berkley Books, 1999)

This very positive book, written by a stepgrandmother, is surprisingly insightful into the basics of stepfamily life. The author takes a refreshing and mature approach to stepfamily issues, focusing on solutions, not excuses. She discusses how to help children adapt to their two homes, stressing that they must feel like part of the family, rather than visitors, in the non-custodial home. The book includes helpful stories from stepparents, practical guidance on money matters, school issues, and family customs, and a valuable section for stepgrandparents. It also identifies twelve stumbling blocks that stepparents should avoid and lists twelve secrets to successful blending. **Best:** The information on understanding and reducing stress in your life.

The Courage To Be A Stepmom: Finding Your Place Without Losing Yourself by Sue Patton Thoele (Wildcat Canyon Press, 1999)

The author, a psychotherapist and stepmother, begins this comforting book by helping readers understand the impact of the past and present on their families. She stresses the need for flexibility as stepmoms search for the courage to be "teachers of love and connection." The eight concise "stepmuddling" steps are a practical guide for getting through typical stepfamily struggles. "Gathering the Gifts," an inspirational section, discusses the gifts we receive from stepchildren and the spiritual gifts that we might not develop as fully in a different family situation. **Best:** Twenty Guidelines for Stepmothers.

The "Disengaging" Essay (author unknown). It appears on several websites, including: *http://www.steptogether.org/disengaging.shtml* and *http://www.secondwivesclub.com/disengage1.shtml*

This piece has become a classic among stepmoms whose stepchildren do not respect them and whose husbands are not supportive. It recommends that the stepmom disengage— that is, regain control of her life by turning responsibility for her stepkids over to their dad, and it lists ten "realities" that she must accept in order to do that. Although disengaging isn't easy, the essay provides examples and points out its benefits, for both stepmoms and their husbands.

The Enlightened Stepmother: Revolutionizing the Role by Perdita Kirkness Norwood with Teri Wingender (Avon Books, Inc., 1999)

An open and honest look at a stepmom's life, including the often-overlooked rights and responsibilities of her role. Each area is covered in depth, including variations on almost every circumstance. The author stresses that it's important for a stepmom to explore her emotions and honestly admit how she feels about her new life. Topics include unrealistic expectations, the stages of stepfamily life, building a strong marriage while understanding your husband's unique challenges, dealing with all ages of stepchildren, and more. There's also a very helpful "Stepmom's Legal File." **Best:** "Action Box" pages throughout the text provide practical, immediate suggestions for dealing with an issue.

Inner Simplicity: 100 Ways to Regain Peace and Nourish Your Soul by Elaine St. James (Hyperion, 1995)

The author says that "inner simplicity means getting rid of the extraneous things—such as worry and anger and judgment—that get in the way of having peace and tranquility in our lives." That's especially true for stepmoms, who have more than their share of heavy issues to deal with. This book is brief and a pleasure to read, starting out easy and then challenging the reader to make positive changes. **Best:** Figuring out your "big issue."

It's Not My Stepkids—It's Their Mom! by Karon Phillips Goodman (EquiLibrium Press, 2002)

A quick guide to help stepmoms find solutions for dealing with a difficult ex-wife/mother of her stepchildren. Subjects include understanding her motives, documentation, what to do when your husband is weak, and Parental Alienation Syndrome. Published as an e-book.

Keys to Successful Stepmothering by Philippa Greene Mulford (Barron Educational Series, 1996)

This packed book offers quick, practical information generously peppered with real-life stepmom stories that are both enlightening and inspiring. It covers a wide range of topics, including the second wedding, stepsiblings, money, discipline, the ex-wife, and lots of common sense ways to help yourself in a variety of situations. **Best:** Stepchildren's Advice to Stepmothers.

Positive Discipline for Your Stepfamily: Nurturing Harmony, Respect, and Joy in Your New Family by Jane Nelson, Ed.D., Cheryl Erwin, M.A., and H. Stephen Glenn, Ph.D. (Prima Publishing, 2000)

This book contains a lot of good, practical information, presented in a plain, easy to read format. It covers how to understand loyalty, work through common differences, and put positive discipline to work. It also includes ways of building new traditions and creating a new family identity. **Best:** Facing your own responsibility to your marriage.

The Second Wives Club by Lenore Fogelson Millian, Ph.D., and Stephen Jerry Millian, Ph.D. (Beyond Words Publishing, Inc., 1999)

This book focuses on stepmothers who have their own children. The author relates several clinical examples of stepmoms in therapy, noting how they deal with such issues as unconscious needs and their impact on the marriage. There are helpful quizzes at the end of each chapter. **Best:** Help Yourself Tools in the final chapter.

Stepfamilies Stepping Ahead: An 8-Step Program for Successful Family Living by Emily Visher, Ph.D., and John Visher, Ph.D. (Stepfamily Association of America, Inc., 2000)

This easy-to-read handbook by the founders of the Stepfamily Association of America helps stepparents understand how their families are different from traditional families. The book offers eight tasks that every stepfamily needs to complete to create a new identity. This system is easy to apply to any family. **Best:** The Stages in Becoming a Stepfamily—how to understand where you are and what to expect.

Step Wise: A Parent-Child Guide to Family Mergers by James Dale and Alex Beth Shapiro (Andrews McMeel Publishing, 2001)

This slim book, written by a stepfather/stepdaughter team, includes forty-five suggestions to help stepparents learn to relax and accept their stepchildren. It's tongue-in-cheek much of the time, but the basic truth is there, too: stepparents have to earn their stepchildren's love, and a good attitude is crucial. **Best:** The suggestions for understanding and patience are helpful if the reader has kids of her own, too.

Striving for Peace: Managing Conflict in Non-Custodial Homes by Nicole L. Weyant (Weyant Press, 2001)

The author writes of a deeply personal struggle that she and her husband faced and gives practical advice to help with a situation that is far too common. She clearly explains Malicious Mother Syndrome and Parental Alienation Syndrome (PAS), two extremely damaging yet widespread tactics that custodial parents often inflict upon their children and former spouses. The book helps non-custodial parents understand their responsibilities to the former spouse and provides some enlightening guidelines for divorced parents. **Best:** The extremely detailed chapters on documentation and legalese for parents who are victims of PAS.

Wonderful Ways to Be a Stepparent by Judy Ford and Anna Chase (Conari Press, 1999)

This little gem contains more than sixty suggestions for stepmoms who are trying to grow in their role. The experiences and suggestions are practical and encouraging, and you'll respond to the stories with warm familiarity—or wish they could be your own. ***Best:*** How to Use Your Intuition.

Stepfamily Resources

Stepfamily Association of America
650 J Street, Suite 205
Lincoln, Nebraska 68508
(800) 735-0329
http://www.saafamilies.org

A national organization with many local chapters that is dedicated to providing support and guidance to stepfamilies. Membership includes a copy of "Stepfamilies Stepping Ahead" (see Bibliography) and the quarterly newsletter, *SAA Families*. SAA helps members find or create local support groups and offers personal advice from professionals.

Bonus Families
http://www.bonusfamilies.com

This very positive website, operated by a first and second wife, focuses on the relationships and growth of all stepfamily members. The goal in a bonus family is to feel appreciated for who you are, even if you're not biologically related to everyone in the family. The site features original articles and Bonus Experts to write to for help. Sections include "ex"-etiquette, how to help teens, bonus grandparents, and more.

The "been there, done that" section features stories submitted by readers.

Bride Again Magazine
http://www.brideagain.com

This is the only magazine devoted to encore brides and their families. Updated monthly, it covers etiquette and choices for encore weddings, adjusting to stepchildren, legal and religious issues, financial concerns, advice from experts, and more.

Family Fusion
http://www.familyfusion.com

"Where blended families come together." In this comprehensive site, you'll find articles, message boards, chat, a newsletter, research and statistics, a question and answer page, and more. You can share your own stepparenting story, too.

Parenting Toolbox
http://www.parentingtoolbox.com

This site covers all kinds of tools for parenting (discipline, anger, etc.) and addresses Power Tools for Nontraditional Families. Includes articles, forums, and live counseling. The site features Family Engineers on topics such as stepfamilies, adoption, legal issues, transitions, child behavior, and more. There are self-study classes, seminars, and free teleclasses, as well as a newsletter and online journals that are free to all members.

Second Wives Club
http://www.secondwivesclub.com

Established in 1997, this is the original online community dedicated to stepmoms and second wives. It provides a large and constantly expanding library of articles and original columns on all aspects of steplife. An active forum of stepmoms dispenses lots of advice and encouragement. You'll also find a newsletter, book reviews, chat, and more.

Self Help for Her
http://www.selfhelpforher.com

Self Help for Her is about creating better health, closer relationships, personal success, and greater serenity for your life. Sections of this website include time management, mind and spirit, personal growth, parenting, organization, and inner journeys. The site provides practical strategies for dealing with real-life obstacles to achieving inner balance. There is an inspiring weekly *Insight* Newsletter plus book reviews, de-stress zone, forum, and more.

Separated Parenting Access & Resource Center
http://www.deltabravo.net/custody

SPARC works on behalf of non-custodial parents with an extensive library of tools and free downloads covering all kinds of situations. You'll find evaluation guides, time trackers, legal information, helpful links, and more. An excellent resource.

Stepfamilies UK
http://www.stepfamilies.co.uk

This interactive online magazine is built and maintained by a stepfamily in the United Kingdom. You can discuss your problems with other struggling stepparents, share your stories, visit the forum, or chat. There's a kids' section, too.

Stepfamily Australia and Stepfamily Association of South Australia Inc.
P.O. Box 1162
Gawler, South Australia 5118
(08) 8522 7007
http://www.stepfamily.asn.au

This non-profit organization serves to actively promote the positive aspects of stepfamily life. The founders believe that providing appropriate information is the first step toward successful stepfamily life. The website includes a newsletter, articles, resources, and links to other Australian organizations. Counseling is available online or via email.

Stepfamily Day
http://pages.ivillage.com/christyb37/StepfamilyDay/index.html

The SAA's Stepfamily Activities Coordinator, Christy Borgeld, founded National Stepfamily Day in 1999 to honor the love and dedication of the stepfamily, whose members make a tremendous effort to strengthen the values of their families. Stepfamily Day is recognized throughout the U.S. as a way to help create strong family structures that support individual family members and instill in them a sense of responsibility to others in the family.

Stepfamily Foundation
333 West End Avenue
New York, New York 10023
(212)877-3244
http://www.stepfamily.org

This oldest of stepfamily organizations, founded in 1975, provides various avenues for counseling as well as an extensive library of books and audio tapes. The Foundation also trains stepparents to coach other stepparents and assists in the establishment of support groups.

Stepfamily InFormation
675 Lake Street #249
Oak Park, Illinois 60301
(708) 848-0909
http://www.stepfamilyinfo.org

This packed site has articles to help resolve common problems in stepfamily relationships. In the Stepfamily Issues Forum, we can learn key life skills and take a quiz to learn more about ourselves. You'll find twelve ways to promote health and fulfillment in your marriage and family and prevent failure, along with links to many other resources.

StepFamily Matters
http://step-family-matters.com

At this site, the "Non-Custodial Family's Home on the Net," you'll find a newsletter, message boards, articles, questions and answers, chat, and more. Send in your questions to the "Bonus Mom" and the "Estranged Dad."

The Stepfamily Network
http://www.stepfamily.net

The Stepfamily Network is a nonprofit organization dedicated to educating and supporting stepfamily members so that they can achieve harmony and mutual respect in their lives. The website offers book reviews, articles, research opportunities, a forum, advice, and more.

Stepmothers' Advocacy Group
http://www.stepmothersadvocate.com

The mission statement says it all: to recognize and support the contributions and challenges of stepmothers and to elevate the status of the stepmother in her family, her community and her society. The group seeks to dispel the myth of the "wicked stepmother" with education and support, offering meetings and workshops in Fort Collins, Colorado.

Acknowledgments

Although this book began as a way to help others, it became an unexpected blessing to me. I will be eternally grateful to all of the wonderful people who are now in my life because of it. They will always hold a special place in my heart.

I want to thank all of the devoted stepmoms who have shared their stories here. My thanks go out to Angie, Ann, Brenda, Brenda, Charlene, Cindy, Debbie, Denise, Heidi, Isabella, Janet, Jennifer, Jenny, Jessy, Jodi, Judy, Karen, Kathi, Kelly, Kim, Lucinda, Mendi, Michele, Mikki, Nancy, Polly, Rhonda, Shauna, Theresa, Tracey, Vicki, and to those who did not want their names listed. May you be inspired by their wisdom and compassion. Thanks, also, to my friends and colleagues who have given generously of their time and attention to read the manuscript and share their kind words and enthusiasm.

There are many people who have helped me and supported me in my efforts to write this book and reach other stepmoms, and I am so very grateful. I want to thank Beth Reed Ramirez, the first publisher who believed in my stepfamily writing; Susie Michelle Cortright, a true friend who remains a heartfelt source of inspiration and encouragement; Christy Borgeld, the most dedicated advocate of stepfamilies I've ever known; Dr. Jeannette Lofas and Dr. Barry Miller of the Stepfamily Foundation, whose admiration and respect were both unexpected and strengthening; Peter Gerlach, whose time, insight, and support I greatly appreciate; and BB Webb, my true "sister in all things step." I also am indebted to those webmasters who allowed me to share my work on their sites: Susan Wilkins, Tom Wohlmut, Ron Huxley, Kim Peterson, and Nikki Weyant.

I've received lots of e-mail from stepmoms during the past few years. I want to thank all who trusted me with the intimate details of their lives and responded to me with warmth and caring. To those who wrote with kind comments about my work or an answer to a question, I am grateful and humbled by your support. I especially want to thank Mikki Forsyth, one of those stepmoms I met online long ago. Mikki told me right away that I should write a book for stepmoms. Her enthusiasm has helped me more than she knows.

Finally, I want to thank my publisher, Susan D. Goland of EquiLibrium Press, for her untiring dedication to this book, for her patience and professionalism, and for teaching me that the only thing harder than writing is re-writing! Her sense of humor and unfailing spirit guided me gently through the tough times, and once just my publisher, she is now my friend.

About the Author

Karon Phillips Goodman is a freelance journalist who frequently writes on stepfamily issues. She edits an online newsletter, *The Stepparenting Journey,* and writes a monthly column, "The Stepmom's Sideroom," for *Momscape.com.* She is a frequent contributor to *Bride Again* magazine, and her work also has appeared in *Woman's Day, Writer's Digest, The Writing Parent, Women's Circle,* and numerous other publications and websites.

Karon is the author of an e-book for stepmothers, *It's Not My Stepkids—It's Their Mom!* (EquiLibrium Press, 2002), two e-books for children, a gift book titled *Everyday Angels,* and *You're Late Again, Lord! The Impatient Woman's Guide to God's Timing* (both from Barbour Publishing).

Karon has been a stepmother since 1996. She lives with her husband, son, and (often) two stepsons. When she has the time, she loves to garden, sew, and paint floorcloths and murals.

Read more of Karon's work at *www.karongoodman.com.*

Also from EquiLibrium Press

It's Not My *Stepkids*—It's Their *Mom!*

by Karon Phillips Goodman

This e-book addresses many stepmoms' #1 concern: dealing with their stepchildren's mother. The relationship may be awkward or tense—or it may be downright hostile. Whatever your situation, this practical, positive guide will help you find solutions.
Available online at *www.equipress.com*

"I refer to it a lot and it's one of the best resources I have found."
—Lisa Ball

"I thought my marriage was doomed, but after reading this book, I began to find peace in my soul. My heart was again alive."
—A stepmom from Hawaii

A *Special Delivery:*
Mother-Daughter Letters From Afar

by Joyce Slayton Mitchell & Elizabeth Dix Mitchell

Intimate, inspiring letters between a traditional Yankee mother and her free-spirited daughter, pregnant and living in an idyllic corner of New Zealand. And all of it is true.

"This is a tale to grip the emotions of mothers and grandmothers." — *Vermont Sunday Magazine*

"A fascinating glimpse into the relationship between two women with very different approaches to life—approaches that nonetheless do not get in the way of the bond they share." — *ForeWord* Magazine

"A gift to all who seek a better understanding of families. . . . a rare and memorable treat." —Professor Hope Jensen Leichter, Columbia University

Order Form

Telephone orders: (877) ELPRESS *(Toll-free:* 877-357-7377)
Outside the US: 310-204-3290 ❖ *Fax orders:* (310) 204-3550
❖ *On-line orders: www.equipress.com*
❖ *Postal orders:* EquiLibrium Press, Inc.
10736 Jefferson Blvd. #680
Culver City, CA 90230   USA

___ copies: **The Stepmom's Guide to Simplifying Your Life ($14.00)**

___ copies: **A Special Delivery: Mother-Daughter Letters From Afar ($12.95)**

Ship to:

Name: _____

Address: _____

City: _____ State/Province:_____

Zip/Postal Code: _____Country: _____

Telephone: (___)_____ E-mail: _____

Add 8.25% sales tax for books shipped to California addresses.

Free Shipping within the United States. Allow 10 days for delivery.
International Customers: Call or e-mail for shipping rates.

Payment: Check enclosed Visa   MasterCard   American Express

Credit card number:_____

Name on card: _____ Exp. Date: _____

Last 3 digits on back of credit card (Visa, AmEx only):_____

Call toll free and order now!